HEAR THAT TRAIN WHISTLE BLOW!
How the Railroad Changed the World

LANDMARK BOOKS®

HEAR THAT TRAIN WHISTLE BLOW!
— How the Railroad Changed the World —

MILTON MELTZER

RANDOM HOUSE 🏠 NEW YORK

Copyright © 2004 by Milton Meltzer
All rights reserved under International and Pan-American Copyright Conventions.
Published in the United States by Random House Children's Books, a division of Random House, Inc.,
New York, and simultaneously in Canada by Random House of Canada Limited, Toronto.

www.randomhouse.com/kids

Library of Congress Cataloging-in-Publication Data
Meltzer, Milton.
Hear that train whistle blow! : how the railroad changed the world / by Milton Meltzer.
p. cm. — (Landmark books)
Includes bibliographical references and index.
SUMMARY: Takes a look at the history of rail transportation,
focusing on how it transformed societies from isolated communities that
rarely communicated or traded into unified nations.
ISBN 0-375-81563-5 (trade) — ISBN 0-375-91563-X (lib. bdg.) — ISBN 0-375-82922-9 (pbk.)
1. Railroads—United States—History—Juvenile literature.
2. Railroads—Social aspects—United States—Juvenile literature.
3. Railroads—History—Juvenile literature. 4. Railroads—Social aspects—Juvenile literature.
[1. Railroads—History. 2. Railroads—Social aspects.] I. Title. II. Series.
HE2751.M395 2004   385'.0973'09034—dc22   2003013255

Printed in the United States of America   10 9 8 7 6 5 4 3 2 1   First Edition

RANDOM HOUSE and colophon and LANDMARK BOOKS and colophon are registered trademarks of Random House, Inc.

Photo credits are on page 147.

For Judith and Stanley

Contents

HEAR THAT TRAIN WHISTLE BLOW!
— How the Railroad Changed the World —

Elevated railway, part of New York City's rapid transit system.

Foreword

ONLY A GENERATION OR TWO AGO, ALMOST EVERYONE TRAVELED by train. Probably your mom and dad, and certainly your grandparents. They took it for granted. Railroad trains crisscrossed America, penetrating every corner of the land, every part of the whole wide world. They still do.

It was out of the Industrial Revolution, in the early 1800s, that the railroad was born. Its invention led to the greatest change in human history since people began farming about twelve thousand years ago.

Think what that introduction of agriculture meant. It freed people from having to wander everywhere in search of food. Before the invention of farming, people lived in tribes and got their food by hunting, fishing, and gathering wild plants. Most of the time, primitive people were hungry; they spent all their waking hours searching for food. Few of them ever reached the age of twenty-five.

But when people learned to farm—to sow seeds and take care of the plants until they could be eaten as food—they could stop roaming around and could stay in one place. Here they grew their food, raised livestock, and began to live together in villages, towns, and cities. And thus they created a civilization. This same process went on all over the world.

When prehistoric people made that great leap from nomadic life to settled agriculture, did they realize how so much in existence would change because of it?

So, too, no one would have guessed, more than 175 years ago, what a powerful influence the invention of the railroad would have on our lives. John F. Stover, the dean of American railroad historians, holds that since their appearance in America, railroads have played a decisive role in nearly every major movement in American history. Though people now can move almost anywhere by car or plane, the railroad is still one of the most vital forces in civilization. Freight trains haul more tonnage than ever before. Passenger trains, too, are no less important in many parts of America and around the world. To cite just one example: Commuter lines bring 750,000 people into and out of New York City every day. And the subway trains? New York's system carries 4 million people each day.

This is a mythic story of the past and how it shapes our present. It's a story of legendary personalities and events, of brilliant inventors and idealistic dreamers, of politicians honest and politicians corrupt, of financiers and engineers, of disasters natural and man-made. And especially of the often heroic people who built the trains, laid down the tracks, flung bridges across chasms, tunneled under rivers and through mountains, ran the trains, and served their passengers.

Chapter 1

GETTING AROUND—SLOWLY

THE FIRST RAILROAD IN AMERICA BEGAN OPERATING IN 1827.

How did people get around before then?

The answer: with difficulty and very little. For most people, life centered around country neighborhoods of a dozen or two farms. Few traveled beyond their neighborhood except for an occasional trip to an artisan's shop, a store, a tavern, or a church in a nearby village.

The 1830 census reported a population of only 13 million in the entire country. Today that is the population of the state of Pennsylvania.

Most people traveled primarily on foot. In New England towns, district schools were placed so that four- and five-year-old pupils would walk up to two miles each way. Young people who worked away from home as farm laborers or schoolteachers might walk ten miles to spend Sunday with their families.

Surely, though, there were horses to get people about? Yes, but in colonial times, saddle horses were for the gentry. The expense of buying and keeping horses was too steep for the ordinary American. Besides, cattle, sheep, and pigs were more useful than horses were to farmers and villagers. Horses were used mostly as pack animals, for riding, and later to pull wagons and stage-coaches.

A STAGECOACH DELIVERS MAIL AND PASSENGERS TO AN INN IN COLONIAL VIRGINIA.

In the mid-1700s, a heavier breed of horse was imported and put to hard work. They were hitched to giant wagons to carry freight overland. Throughout the American Revolution, teams of such horses hauled commissary and artillery supplies in the service of George Washington's army.

Later, the huge wagons carried the early pioneers west on the new turn-pikes. As travelers went beyond the Appalachians into the Midwest, the covered wagons were slimmed down for faster passage of families across the prairies. Called prairie schooners, they opened up vast territory—not only in America, but in Australia and South Africa—to migrating peoples.

This was the heyday of the teamsters. Much like today's long-haul truck drivers, teamsters ruled the roads linking American cities. They carried boxes, crates, barrels, and bales on their big wagons. And they moved their heavy loads slowly. It took a six-horse team hauling a four-ton load all day to cover twenty-five miles.

Passenger traffic moved in stagecoaches. Their lines connected cities on a regular schedule. Again, slowly! To travel the one hundred miles between Philadelphia and New York, it took three days. Travel sped up when four horses were used instead of two; they cut the same run to forty-eight hours.

Of course, people and goods moved by ship, too. They sailed along the seacoast and on the many rivers that penetrated the country. Boats were also hauled along canals that had been dug in a few places.

But up until the early nineteenth century, the horse was still the primary means of travel.

Then came the railroad—an invention no one dreamed would create enormous changes in the way people lived.

Chapter 2

A BETTER WAY

TRAINS ARE WHEELED VEHICLES THAT RUN ON TRACKS MADE OF rails. That's why we have the words "railway" and "railroad." The railed tracks were created long before the engine and the cars it hauls. The use of railways goes far back in time. The earliest railway appeared in England in 1630, soon after the poet and playwright William Shakespeare died. It was used for hauling coal from a mining pit. Horses, mules, or humans drew the coal wagons along tracks made of wood.

Wood rails didn't wear well under heavy weights. By 1740 rails molded of iron came into use; they proved superior to wood. In 1780 a cast-edge railway that took a flanged wheel was introduced. Soon edged rails, narrow at the base and widened toward the top, were being manufactured.

By the early 1800s, machinery was developed that could roll rails into a shape much like that used today. But the rails were only three or four feet in length, requiring that they be joined together. Around the same time, methods of track construction were being improved, with stone props placed beneath the rails at the points where they were joined.

This was the time in England and America when the industrial production of goods was getting under way. As markets expanded, business tried to

Horse-drawn coal wagon on rails.

speed up the distribution of raw materials and manufactured products. That was a tall order, especially for America, a country of huge size compared with the nations of Europe. As people on the eastern seaboard began to move westward, many obstacles to transport had to be surmounted. Waterways ran mostly north–south; a natural east–west system was almost completely lacking. Wagon shipments to settlers in the Midwest seemed to take forever.

Enterprising people became aware of an urgent need for a better transportation network.

The obvious way to open the West to settlement and trade was to build roads. A beginning was made. But by the 1820s, it was clear that horse-drawn wagons alone couldn't get raw materials rapidly to the factories where they were needed, or get products to the markets where they could be sold. That need for cheap transport of ever more abundant goods led to improvements in ports, canals, and bridges as well as roads.

It was in England that the solution to rapid transport was born. The problem was to develop an engine that would replace animal power to haul loads along a railway. It had to be an engine that could be built by practical men and that would not only work but also be profitable.

The introduction of the steam engine was a step-by-step process. That's generally true of most inventions. No sooner is some new mechanism or material developed to meet a need than new ideas or extensions to other possibilities—once believed impossible or simply unthought of—become possible.

A LONG TRAIL

THE trail of discovery and innovation that led to the steam engine and then its powering of the locomotive touched the lives of many men. Anyone who wants to trace that path can look up these people who, in succession, built on the work done before them: Captain Savery, Thomas Newcomen, Joseph Black, James Watt, Matthew Boulton, Richard Trevithick, George Stephenson.

British historian of science J. D. Bernal put it this way: "The steam engine, first developed for pumping, was adapted next to blowing furnaces and hammering iron, and then to supplant the water-wheel in driving machinery. Later still, mounted on a boat or wagon, it became automotive and gave birth to the steamship and railway."

It's interesting to note that the engineers credited for so many industrial advances in the eighteenth and nineteenth centuries often began as working mechanics—skillful and ambitious, but usually illiterate or self-taught.

Take, for example, Englishman George Stephenson. As a child in a poor mining family, he

GEORGE STEPHENSON (1781–1848), BUILDER OF THE FIRST STEAM LOCOMOTIVE.

watched trains of horse-drawn wagons hauling coal. At fifteen he got a job as a fireman on a mine's steam-pump engine, learning all he could about how the engine worked and how to repair it. At eighteen he went to night school to learn to read and write. In 1814 he built a traveling engine to haul coal from mines. A year later, he built his first steam locomotive, the Blucher, the most successful one of that time. His many innovations earned him fame in England and America.

On both sides of the Atlantic in this era, the movers of the Industrial Revolution were bent on inventing better ways of making and doing things. These mechanics demonstrated the kind of practical ingenuity that we see in the clockmaker or locksmith. They appreciated the needs of their time and sensed where labor might be saved and profits increased.

Oliver Evans, a Philadelphia experimenter, was one of those farsighted men. As early as 1813, he predicted the time when "carriages propelled by steam will be in general use." They would travel over their own selected routes, "almost as fast as birds fly, 15 or 20 miles an hour," traveling on double tracks so that the "carriages may pass each other in different directions, and travel by night as well as by day; and the passengers will sleep in the stages as comfortably as they now do in steam boats."

Chapter 3

THEY DID IT

Since railroads proved useful around coal mines, why not try them to connect cities? In 1825 George Stephenson took the lead in England by hauling six hundred people from Darlington to Stockton in some three hours, including stops. His success proved that passenger coaches on a train worked well. Within a month, regular passenger service began.

Bigger ventures were soon in the planning. Investors thought a link between the great cotton port of Liverpool and the cotton-manufacturing center of Manchester would be profitable. The directors set standards and then offered a cash prize for the best locomotive to meet the requirements of such a line. Thousands of spectators assembled on October 6, 1829, at the town of Rainhill, near Liverpool, to watch five locomotives and their builders compete. Stephenson brought in his newly designed locomotive, the Rocket, and it beat all four competitors on every one of the eight conditions set.

It was a great day for modern railroading. Among the spectators were two Americans, Horatio Allen and E. L. Miller, representing railroad companies. The United States had already seen its first railroad, in 1827. It ran from the granite quarries of Quincy, Massachusetts, to the Neponset River, a three-mile length. That same year another railroad, nine miles long, built in

THE ROCKET, A STEPHENSON LOCOMOTIVE.

Pennsylvania, carried coal from the mines in Carbondale to barges on the Lehigh River. Both rail lines were built on wooden rails bound with strap iron set on wooden sleepers.

Getting railroads started in America wasn't easy. Early on, politicians and investors promoted canal and highway projects to develop the inner continent. Railroads? Their value was yet to be proved. Why pour public or private money into them? There was a selfish motive, too, in the resistance to railroading. Turnpike and canal operators, tavern keepers, and freight handlers all feared their livelihood would be threatened by a shift to steam locomotion.

Then, too, it horrified some people to think of hurtling along a track at a speed of fifteen or twenty miles an hour. Wasn't that a sinful departure from the Lord's plan for us?

The historian Seymour Dunbar quotes a newspaper columnist of 1830 predicting (tongue in cheek?) what the introduction of the railroad would do:

> It will set the whole world a-gadding. . . . Grave, plodding citizens will be flying about like comets. All local attachments will be at an end. It will encourage flightiness of intellect. Veracious people will turn into the most immeasurable liars. All conceptions will be exaggerated by the magnificent notions of distance. . . . It will upset

A POSTER CIRCULATED IN PHILADELPHIA IN 1839 TO ROUSE PUBLIC PROTEST AGAINST THE COMING OF THE RAILROAD.

all the gravity of the nation. . . . Upon the whole, sir, it is a
pestilential, topsy-turvy, harum-scarum whirligig. . . . None of
your hop, and jump whimsies for me.

Still, there was a modest beginning, and venturesome railroad builders
picked up speed.

In South Carolina, Horatio Allen, who had witnessed the Rocket's victory in England, induced the local railroad company to use steam power on
the new line being laid out of Charleston. On Christmas Day 1830, an early
locomotive built in the United States—called Best Friend of Charleston—
hauled 141 passengers on the first scheduled steam railroad line in America.
By 1833 its 136-mile route to Hamburg was completed. Now Carolina had the
largest continuous railroad in the world.

Hoping for more commercial business, Boston merchants financed three
short lines in the 1830s. One linked Boston and Lowell, another Boston and
Providence, and the last, Boston and Worcester. The third was pushed farther
west, to Springfield, and then through the Berkshires to the Hudson River
and Albany.

By 1833 rail passengers could travel between Philadelphia and New
York—a seven-hour run—for three dollars.

By 1840 the United States had laid more miles of track than Great Britain.
At a cost of $75 million, three thousand miles of track were built. Of the
twenty-six states in 1840, only four had not built their first mile of track.
Two-thirds of the trackage was in the North; the South claimed only eleven
hundred miles of track.

Inventive Americans borrowed from the technical achievements developed in Britain and improved on them at a faster pace. By 1850 railroads had
climbed over the Appalachian Mountains. In a boom never before seen, over
thirty thousand miles of track were built by 1860, more than in the rest of

ENGINEERS

THE word "engineer" is used often in these pages. What does it mean? Originally it had only military meaning, referring to the man who built and worked the engines of war: the catapult, the storming tower, the fortification of camps. In Europe of the 1700s, its meaning was expanded to include builders of canals, bridges, and wharves. Still, the engineer was not ranked in the learned professions. He was considered just a highly skilled craftsman. Even if you invented and built a new machine, you were called a mechanic.

In America in the early 1800s, men with inventive talent, like Eli Whitney and Robert Fulton, pioneered in their fields but won little respect. Although the right to patent your invention was written into the first article of the U.S. Constitution, inventions were pirated left and right, and the courts did little to provide protection.

It took a long time for the profession of engineering to gain standing. Britain had no professional society until 1818, and the United States, not until 1852. The first school in the United States to offer an engineering education was the U.S. Military Academy at West Point, in 1817. There were but few others for many decades. Gradually engineering proliferated, with many subdivisions: civil, mechanical, electrical, chemical, aeronautical, industrial, computer, mineral, genetic— and railroad.

NIGHT SCENE IN THE CAB OF A STEAM LOCOMOTIVE, WITH THE ENGINEER AT THE CONTROLS AND THE FIREMAN SHOVELING COAL.

the world's countries combined. Railways now stretched as far west as the Mississippi River.

Private capital financed most of the railroads. But many cities, states, and the federal government provided vital aid with loans, land grants, and guarantees of bond issues. These investments were a powerful spur to economic growth. The railroads reduced the time and costs of transportation, and that helped to develop an interregional market economy.

When a manufacturer shipped freight from Cincinnati to New York in 1817, it took over fifty days to arrive. By 1852, only six days. For passengers making the same trip, the time was cut from three weeks to two days.

It was a profitable change for both producer and consumer. Western farmers could now send their products east by train, and for a price families could afford to pay. Between 1818 and 1858, the wholesale price of western pork dropped from $1.53 to $1.18 a barrel. A barrel of western flour slid from $2.48 to 28 cents during the same period.

With access to a national market through the spread of the railroad, farmers and manufacturers could reduce their unit costs as they reached a greater number of customers. As farmers quadrupled their output in the four decades before the Civil War, they were able to feed the rapidly increasing population of the cities.

Of course this was not due solely to the railroads. Before 1800 American farmers did their work much as farmers had done back in biblical times. But in the first half of the nineteenth century, a host of inventors developed implements and machines that revolutionized agriculture.

The leap in technology was just as true of American manufacturing. Household production of handcrafted goods for family use and for local markets gave way to shop- and factory-produced goods that reached regional and national markets.

By the 1840s, America was no longer closely bound to advances in European technology. It was in the United States that the greatest contribution to the Industrial Revolution was made—the mass production of machine-made interchangeable parts. It began with the manufacture of firearms in the early 1800s, when Eli Whitney, a small-town boy from New England, a blacksmith in his youth, developed the revolutionary innovation of identical interchangeable parts. Gradually his system of mass production expanded to include dozens of products: clocks and watches, boots and shoes, nails, screws, nuts and bolts, locks, and even parts for steam engines and locomotives.

There were two basic reasons for America's rapid modernization. One was the high level of mass education and literacy. The other was the openness to change, the willingness always to try something new, something better. The one fed into the other.

Take education, for example: In 1850 the United States had the highest literacy rate (89 percent) and the highest percentage of children in school of any country in the world except for Sweden and Denmark. Not counting the slave population. No wonder, said a British study, that "the American working boy develops

ELI WHITNEY, AT ABOUT AGE FIFTY.

rapidly into the skilled artisan, and having mastered one part of the business, he is never content until he has mastered all."

Every working boy in New England seemed to have an idea for some mechanical invention or improvement in manufacturing. Take Elias Howe, for example, the Boston machinist who invented the sewing machine.

The other factor—the thirst for innovation—came out of the heritage of revolution and freedom. Unlike Europeans—whose tradition of monarchy and aristocracy predisposed them to accept things as they were—Americans felt they were a new and unique people. They looked to the future, not to the past; they valued change more than tradition; they believed in "progress" and "improvement."

This enthusiasm for the new went so far as to value machines themselves as agents of moral improvement and democratic equality. The railroads, declared one man, are God's instrument "to quicken the activity of men; to send energy and vitality where before were silence and barrenness; to multiply cities and villages, studded with churches, dotted with schools."

ELIAS HOWE (1819–1867).

18

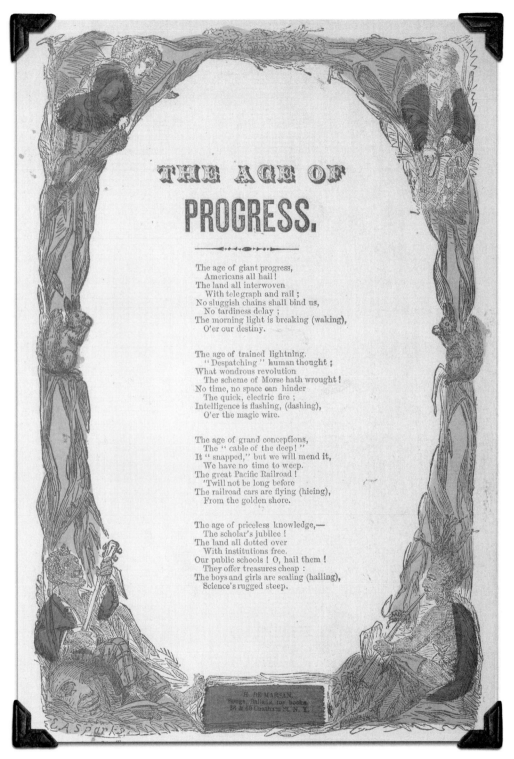

THE AGE OF
PROGRESS.

The age of giant progress,
  Americans all hail!
The land all interwoven
  With telegraph and rail ;
No sluggish chains shall bind us,
  No tardiness delay ;
The morning light is breaking (waking),
  O'er our destiny.

The age of trained lightning.
  "Despatching" human thought ;
What wondrous revolution
  The scheme of Morse hath wrought!
No time, no space can hinder
  The quick, electric fire ;
Intelligence is flashing, (dashing),
  O'er the magic wire.

The age of grand conceptions,
  The "cable of the deep!"
It "snapped," but we will mend it,
  We have no time to weep.
The great Pacific Railroad !
  'Twill not be long before
The railroad cars are flying (hieing),
  From the golden shore.

The age of priceless knowledge,—
  The scholar's jubilee !
The land all dotted over
  With institutions free.
Our public schools ! O, hail them !
  They offer treasures cheap :
The boys and girls are scaling (hailing),
  Science's rugged steep.

H. DE MARSAN,
Songs, Ballads, &c., Books,
38 & 60 Chatham St. N. Y.

A SONG OF 1860 HAILS THE RAILROAD AS ONE OF
THE GREAT CONTRIBUTORS TO PROGRESS.

Chapter 4

C'MON! LET'S GET THERE!

The American continent provided both advantages and disadvantages for the pioneering railroaders. Distances were vast, mountains many and huge, grades steep, curves scarily sharp. But wood to fuel the steam engines was plentiful and cheap. And Americans were notoriously always in a rush: "C'mon! Let's get there!"

At first, steam engines were imported, but as good as they were in Britain, in America they proved to be too massive, too rigid. They did not work well on a different terrain. With their customary ingenuity, American mechanics kept making changes in design, creating better locomotives for the lines springing up everywhere.

The first American steam locomotive was the small Tom Thumb, designed and built by Peter Cooper in 1830 and used on a thirteen-mile track in Maryland. But the first American-built full-size locomotive was created by Matthias Baldwin in 1832. It averaged only a mile an hour, though gradually the speed was pushed up to twenty-eight miles per hour. A great improvement came in 1832 when John B. Jervis designed the first swivel wheels, mounted on a truck under the front of the locomotive. Now all curves could be taken easily, and speeds up to sixty miles per hour achieved. In 1837 an

THE TOM THUMB, AMERICA'S FIRST LOCOMOTIVE TO PULL A LOAD OF PASSENGERS, IN 1830.

eight-wheel engine was introduced that set the pattern for locomotive design for half a century.

That same year, the first locomotive with a steam whistle was used on the Baltimore and Ohio line. The idea was to signal the brakeman and the train crew, as well as to warn pedestrians that a train was approaching. Later, engineers improvised their own special, rhythmic whistle as a kind of

A RAILWAY TRESTLE BUILT OF WOOD,
ON THE NORTHERN PACIFIC LINE.

personal signature. "Hear that whistle? It's Henry on the way!"

Many of the early locomotives were made by the Lowell Machine Shop. It built machine tools for the textile mills in that Massachusetts town. As the railroad system expanded, the shop adapted by making locomotives. Between 1845 and 1854, it produced sixty-one of them. But competition was intense. By 1855 there were forty-four locomotive works in the country. Progress was so rapid that in a matter of months a locomotive design could become obsolete—much like the computers of today. Always in a hurry, the railroad companies built cheap wooden bridges across rivers and gorges. Many a passenger muttered prayers as the train rattled over the shaky structures.

Early on, rail lines were owned and operated by different companies. Each railroad laid down different-gauge tracks to discourage competitors within their area from connecting with their lines. The early roads were usually built to the English gauge of four feet eight and a half inches. But in New York, the Erie Railroad used a broader width of six feet, thinking to prevent loss of traffic to other lines. In the South, a five-foot gauge was common. It would be fifty years before a uniform gauge was achieved.

The early passenger cars were small, each car designed like the stage-coach, with passengers sitting facing each other. By 1831, when Andrew Jackson became the first president to travel by train, corridor-type cars were in use. Fanny Kemble, an English actress touring America by train in 1832, said that passengers fidgeted up and down the center aisle, tobacco chewers spit in it, and fruit and cake sellers rushed through peddling their wares at every stop. Water boys passed through the cars with long-spout cans and a couple of glasses (complete with germs) for the benefit of thirsty travelers.

The average length of the first hundred or so roads was about forty miles. Though the trip was short, passengers didn't expect a comfortable ride. The cars were dirty, crowded, and poorly equipped. English novelist Charles Dickens (1812–1870), visiting America ten years after Fanny Kemble, wrote of the trains he took:

> There is a great deal of jolting, a great deal of noise, a great deal of wall, not much window, a locomotive, a shriek and a bell. The cars are shabby omnibuses, but larger: holding thirty, forty, fifty people. The seats, instead of stretching from end to end, are placed crosswise. In the center of the carriage there is usually a stove, fed with charcoal or

FANNY KEMBLE (1809–1893).

anthracite coal, which is for the most part red-hot. It is insuf-
ferably close; and you can see the hot air fluttering between
yourself and any other object you happen to look at, like the
ghost of smoke. . . . The conductor, or check-taker, or guard, or
whatever he may be, wears no uniform. He walks up and down
the car, and in and out of it, as his fancy dictates; leans against
the door with his hands in his pockets and stares at you . . . or
enters into conversation with the passengers about him.

Travel was strictly one class. A gentleman might find himself packed in
next to who knows who? Not only was he uncomfortable, but his dignity
was dented. Added to discomfort was danger. Another English visitor, writer
Harriet Martineau, suffered thirteen holes burned in her gown by cinders in
just one short ride.

By 1850 trains were snaking into almost every corner of eastern America.
None had yet gone past the Mississippi. But ambition knew no limit.
Periodicals and politicians loudly boasted of America's Manifest Destiny to
carry democracy not only throughout the broad continent but to the whole
wide world. And it was a system of railroads that would accomplish it.

Walt Whitman proclaimed in his poetry that the railroad was the "type
of the modern—emblem of motion and power—pulse of the continent." To
him the shriek of the train whistle evoked a "fierce-throated beauty."

Trains were soon modified to meet changing needs. Headlights were
attached to the prow of the locomotive so trains could travel by night as well
as by day. Competition, the spur of progress, led companies to build cars with
greater comfort, including fully adjustable seats.

The first sleeping cars appeared in the late 1830s, in Baltimore. The local
paper reported, "The cars intended for night traveling between this city and
Philadelphia, and which afford berths for 24 persons in each, have been placed

on the road and will be used for the first time tonight. Nothing seems to be wanting to make railway travel perfect and complete in every convenience."

Not quite true, as Dickens experienced the same American sleeping car: "To tell you that these beds are perfectly comfortable would be a lie."

The irritated novelist wasn't the only one to think the railroads had to do better. In 1857 Theodore T. Woodruff, an inventor, introduced a sleeping car with three tiers of berths. He went into business producing his cars with money supplied by young Andrew Carnegie (1835–1919), an American industrialist.

More importantly, railroad bridges were vastly improved. In place of the wooden trestle came the iron bridge. J. G. Kohl, a mid-century European traveler, was awestruck by the suspension bridge that J. A. Roebling, a German American engineer, had flung across the Niagara River in western New York. The spectacle was almost as astounding as Niagara Falls itself, Kohl wrote.

> For more than ten years men have been spinning like spiders the iron web that connects Canada with the Union; have tried with great labor various experiments and when their work has been destroyed by the powers of Nature, have begun again; and at length triumphed over all obstacles. As the river here is almost as deep as it is broad, the erection of piers was out of the question, and since the river runs at the Narrows with fearful velocity, there could be no bridge of boats. . . . Nothing remained, therefore, but to adopt the plan of the spider, when he flings his fine thread from tree to tree, through the air. Paper kites were prepared, and when the wind was fair for the attempt, sent across, loaded with the first thin wires . . . and now from that first thin, almost invisible wire, we have arrived at a grand and beautiful suspension bridge, that is, perhaps, unequaled in the world. The chains on which it hangs are

ROEBLING'S SUSPENSION BRIDGE ACROSS THE NIAGARA RIVER.

as thick as ships' masts, and more than a thousand feet long, and the towers that support them are masterpieces of modern architecture. They are about 250 feet high, and divided into two stories; through the upper one runs the railroad, and through the lower a broad and spacious roadway for passengers, horsemen, and carriages.

During the boom years after the Civil War, several other railroad bridges were built, spanning the Missouri, Mississippi, and Ohio rivers. The peak achievement of the time, however, was the Brooklyn Bridge, designed by Roebling. Crossing the East River, it linked Manhattan with the then independent town of Brooklyn. Opening in 1883, it became the most famous bridge in the world. Its towers rise 272 feet above the water and are made entirely of granite. Each cable holding the platform in suspension is composed of 5,296 galvanized steel wires. The total length of wire used is 14,357 miles, a distance of more than half the circumference of the globe.

CABLES BEING PUT IN PLACE DURING CONSTRUCTION OF THE BROOKLYN BRIDGE IN THE 1870S.

Chapter 5

IT SEEMED LIKE A DREAM

DURING THE 1830S, AMERICANS EXPERIENCED WITH THE NEW railroad an acceleration of travel and communication they had never known before. Judging by time of travel, the new western settlements were nearer than the colonial frontiers had been.

"I saw today for the first time a railway car," wrote C. C. Baldwin in 1835. "What an object of wonder! How marvelous it is in every particular. It appears like a thing of life. . . . I cannot describe the strange sensation produced on seeing the train of cars come up. And when I started in them it seemed like a dream."

Although only a small proportion of Americans traveled on the early railroads, catching a train to anywhere quickly became a mark of modernity. People loved to try the new and the strange, and they thrilled to the speed of a train hurtling downgrade.

Passenger traffic and the revenue it brought in were more important to the railroads than they are today. Maybe a third of a line's total revenue came from riders. Fares dropped as competition for passengers grew. By 1850 a passenger paid only two and a half to three and a half cents per mile in the northern states, and about five cents in the rest of the country.

Rapid transit on the early railroads offered new pleasure to Americans, but increased risks, too. The steam engines rarely exploded, but trains might run off the rails or collide with other trains and vehicles. Axles and frames could break. Bridges could collapse.

In a head-on collision in 1885, the steam locomotive of one train landed on top of the other.

Disasters were mainly due to negligence and lack of experience. Safety in those decades was not the prominent concern in most minds. Often the train crews knew relatively little about the machines they operated and took chances out of ignorance. It didn't seem to alarm passengers, whose numbers kept growing.

Bigger by far than the profits of passenger traffic was the income from freight. It was cheaper to send goods by rail than by horse and wagon. A shipment on the new Boston–Worcester line cost only a third of the wagon charge. Bad weather or winter ice could close the canals for several months, but the railroads would almost never stop. By the early 1850s, the traffic in livestock, packinghouse products, and general merchandise was heavy and continuous. The railroad was now the dominant power in transportation.

In that decade before the Civil War, American railroads would enjoy one of their greatest periods of expansion. The new invention of the telegraph was used to control the operation of the lines. For the first time, a locomotive moved past the Mississippi to serve pioneers on the far side of the great river. In California the first railroad was built to join Sacramento with Folsom. The Midwest now boasted the first railway over seven hundred miles long—the Illinois Central. By 1860 Chicago was the hub of eleven different railroads. The national system had leaped from nine thousand to over thirty thousand miles.

It was a fantastic rate of growth. What other business operated on so vast a scale or employed so many men with such varied skills? Here was young America, with only 5 percent of the world's population, running rail lines with as much mileage as the rest of the whole world.

What helped mightily was the lobbying railroad men did in Washington, D.C., and the state capitals. With abundant cash, shares of stock, and free railroad passes, the doors were opened to legislative favors. Between 1850 and 1857,

An early view of the Illinois Central Railroad depot in Chicago.

the railroads got 25 million acres of public land, absolutely free, and millions of dollars in loans (through bonds) from the state legislatures. The railroads took advantage of an economic system that was not planned for human need but that developed out of the profit motive. Business interests were always helped, going back to the time of Alexander Hamilton and the first Congress.

What happened in Illinois showed the way. In 1851 the state chartered the Illinois Central and granted it 2.5 million acres. The company raised money by selling the land and paying back the state with 7 percent of its gross income. The line ran north–south down the state's center, with a

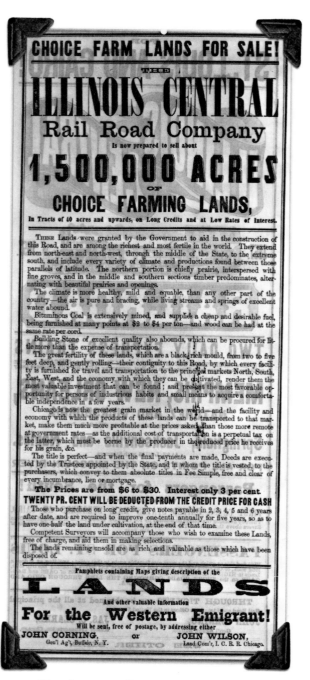

THE ILLINOIS CENTRAL, THE FIRST
LAND-GRANT RAILROAD, USED POSTERS
TO PROMOTE THE SALE OF FARMLAND
GIVEN TO IT BY THE GOVERNMENT.

branch northeast to Chicago. An immense national advertising campaign brought in thousands of people, mostly Irish and German, to build the line as well as to settle the land along the routes. Within ten years, Illinois became a boom state, with the railroad earning high profits.

To achieve stability, and to avoid the costs of frequent depressions, the railroads tried to decrease competition, to organize themselves more rationally, to create mergers, and to move toward monopoly wherever possible. The New York Central line was an example of the merger of many railroads.

Railroads in the South go back to 1830, as we've seen. But construction there lagged behind the rest of the nation for almost a century. A major reason was that the financiers of most lines operated out of the Northeast. They thought very little in the way of profit could be gathered from the plantation economy of the slaveholding South. One of the South's few successful lines was the Louisville and Nashville, linking Atlanta with the river trade on the Ohio.

"Gross fraud and corruption" were often behind the granting of favors to the railroads as well as other business enterprises. "Railroads," Professor Arthur C. Cole goes on, "received legislative favors by methods that varied from political manipulation to sheer bribery." In Wisconsin in 1858, a state investigative committee charged that a railroad bribed the governor with fifty thousand dollars while key assemblymen received five thousand dollars each. Focusing on New York State's legislature, *Harper's Weekly* of June 2, 1860, commented that "votes were openly bought and sold last winter at the state capital." Such corruption reached into the national capital, where "scoundrels looted the public treasury," said Cole.

Expansion of the railroads wasn't always easy or painless. In Michigan, for instance, a rail line ran into trouble with local farmers. The trains sometimes slammed into livestock that failed to leap off the track when the whistle sounded. Although the railroad fenced all its track, somehow animals were still killed. When the line refused to pay the full price of the dead beasts, the farmers and sympathetic townsfolk got even. They tampered with switches, greased rails, and even peppered engines and cars with rocks and buckshot. Finally, when the farmers burned down a depot, the law stepped in. A dozen farmers were sentenced to jail for conspiracy.

It was 1856 when the first railroad bridge was built across the Mississippi. Steamboat lines, losing traffic to the railroad, tried to block it by various legal and physical methods, but Illinois lawyer Abraham Lincoln helped win the case for the railroad.

Lincoln's political rival, Senator Stephen A. Douglas of Illinois, pushed through Congress the first land-grant act to help the railroads expand. The law gave so many acres of land bordering each mile of railroad to the Illinois Central as well as lines in other states. The roads made a nice profit by selling thousands of acres of the land, thus bringing new settlers into the territory the lines served.

By the late 1850s, the best passenger cars were equipped with a corner toilet and water tank. With more and more people traveling at night, several inventors experimented with the design of sleeping cars. George Pullman's won out over the others'. He designed an upper berth that folded into the ceiling during the day, holding the bedding for both upper and lower berths. But dining cars had not yet been introduced. Travelers had to buy snacks hurriedly wherever the train made its scheduled short stops.

As railroad mileage expanded, so did the rate of accidents. As we've seen, tracks were badly maintained, bridges poorly built, staff all too careless. Railroad historian John F. Stover said the motto of the rail executives seemed to be "Let's lay more track and to hell with the maintenance."

No wonder disasters and loss of life became agonizingly frequent. At Norwalk, Connecticut, in 1853, a careless engineer ran the train onto an open drawbridge; forty-six people died. Where two lines crossed, there was often no traffic control, leading that same year to the collision of two trains in Illinois, with eighteen killed and sixty injured. That year alone in America, there were over one hundred accidents; 234 passengers were killed and 496 seriously injured.

Bridges were among the worst hazards. Except for Roebling's bridge near Niagara Falls, most built in the fifties were wooden. Stressed by the constant heavy loads, bridges shattered; as they fell, car stoves ignited the debris. Many people died in the flames.

Accidents were not the only problem for train service. The variety of gauge widths, the lack of transfer facilities, and the absence of bridges across such major rivers as the Potomac and the Ohio meant that physical integration of the rail network was still many years off.

Whatever their limitations, the railroads were a blessing to a rapidly growing nation. They did far more for transport than the earlier improvements: the turnpikes and canals. Still, Americans never stopped dreaming and planning. . . . Why not build a railroad right out to the Pacific?

DICKENS: AN ACCIDENT

IN 1865, just after the American Civil War ended, Charles Dickens experienced the horror of a train wreck in England. He was a passenger on the Folkestone train when it accidentally began to cross a bridge that was under repair. Eight of the fourteen cars plunged from the track into a swampy waterway below. Many people were killed or injured. Dickens's car was caught on part of the bridge and hung suspended in the air. He climbed out carefully and balanced on the car step, looking down into the sheer drop. Hysterical people were jumping through the windows into the swamp.

Dickens managed to get down and set to work trying to help the injured. He had a bottle of brandy with him:

> I stumbled over a lady lying on her back against a pollard tree, with the blood streaming over her face (which was lead-color) in a number of distinct little streams from the head. I asked her if she could swallow a little brandy and she just nodded, and I gave her some and left her for somebody else. The next time I passed her she was dead. [He did not know the probable effects of brandy on cases of bad shock.] Then a man came running up to me and implored me to help him find his wife, who was afterwards found dead. No imagination can conceive the ruin of the carriages or the extraordinary weight under which people were lying, or the complications into which they were twisted up among iron and wood, and mud and water.

Although Dickens behaved with great presence of mind, the aftereffects of the accident, said his son Henry, "left a shock upon his nervous system from which he never quite recovered." He traveled often by train on his reading tours, and whenever there was a slight jolt, he started writhing with fear. On one trip to Scotland he suffered "thirty thousand shocks of the nerves." He died on June 9, 1870, the fifth anniversary of the rail accident.

NOVELIST CHARLES DICKENS
(1812–1870).

Chapter 6

CIVIL WAR

A RAILROAD HEADING WEST TO THE PACIFIC?

It was not a new idea. As far back as the 1840s, Asa Whitney, a New York merchant and China trader, had repeatedly urged Congress to grant a strip of land sixty miles wide from Lake Superior to the Oregon country as the route for building a railway to the Pacific Ocean. His dream would move closer to reality only when young Theodore D. Judah, who had built the first railroad west of the Mississippi, began so passionate a campaign for a transcontinental railroad that it earned him the nickname "Crazy Judah."

Congress agreed the transcontinental was a good idea, but where should the eastern terminus be? Chicago? New Orleans? Memphis? Northerners wanted the route to run through their region; southerners, through theirs. To settle the dispute, Congress in 1853 had the army launch a survey of all feasible routes. Two years later, the thirteen-volume report proposed four routes. It became clear that a staggering sum of money would be needed to carry out any of them. So gigantic an enterprise required federal loans, land grants, financial guarantees. . . .

Before action could be taken, the nation suffered the greatest crisis in its history: the Civil War of 1861–1865. It was a struggle for the future of the

United States. Could the southern states be permitted to secede from the sovereign Union? Could slavery be allowed to exist in a nation born of a declaration that all men are created equal, with the right to life, liberty, and the pursuit of happiness?

By 1861 there was no way around these fundamental issues. One way or another, a solution had to be found. A compromise was impossible.

These great questions would finally be settled—but only in blood.

In 1860, on the eve of the Civil War, America's population numbered 32 million, including 4 million slaves and 4 million foreign-born whites. From their ranks would be drawn the huge armies of the Blue and the Gray.

It was the rapid railway construction of the 1850s that helped create a united North. The East and the West had been sectional rivals early in the railroad era. But the building of connecting lines and the profitable exchange of goods and services during the 1840s and 1850s had created a firm alliance that was able to overpower the South in every way.

As the war began, the rail systems of the two sides stood in sharp contrast. The North had two-thirds of the nation's mileage, five times as many railroad employees, and far more locomotives and passenger and freight cars. On the eve of the Civil War, the South employed over twenty thousand slaves on its railroads.

The demands made on the North's railroads by the war itself led to greater efficiency in both track and bridge construction and closer cooperation among the various lines. The shift from iron to steel rails began in those years, as well as a shift in fuel from wood to coal.

A great handicap for the South was its long history of reliance on the North for most of its railroad equipment. In wartime, that source of supply was cut off. The South's inferior railroads intensified a lack of replacement capacity and produced transportation bottlenecks. The result was frequent

NORTHERN SOLDIERS AWAITING TRANSPORT ON A PLATFORM
OF THE BALTIMORE AND OHIO LINE DURING THE CIVIL WAR.

shortages of food and supplies at the front.

The railroads on both sides were often called on to move great numbers of troops, and to do so quickly. The northern lines proved more able than the southern to carry heavy trainloads of recruits, horses, forage, ordnance, and wounded to and from the battlefields.

Those railroad men—engineers, trainmen, firemen, track builders, car builders, locomotive mechanics—every day of the war risked their lives under the same battle conditions as the soldiers in uniform. They performed almost unbelievable feats reconstructing tracks and bridges in record time.

As the war went on year after year, neither the government of the North nor the South, except for some emergencies, took over its own railroads. The Confederacy never managed to get adequate control over theirs.

Each side tried its best to destroy the lines of the other. Confederate raiders managed to do great damage at times. A few months after the war started, they destroyed fifty of the finest locomotives of the Baltimore and Ohio line, burning them, smashing them with hammers and crowbars, dumping some into the Potomac River.

But because most of the fighting occurred in the South, by far the

UNION AND CONFEDERATE TROOPS BATTLE FOR CONTROL
OF A TRAIN IN VIRGINIA ON JUNE 17, 1861.

greatest damage was done to the Confederate railways. By the end of the war, they were a shambles. The conflict had crippled or destroyed over half the lines. Twisted rails, burned ties, destroyed bridges, gutted depots and shops, and lost or dilapidated rolling stock were the normal heritage of war for most southern lines.

Even after the war ended, some of the southern lines remained out of service for several years. In the North, railroads were mostly in good shape. The needs of war had led to great expansion of the nation's network. Over forty-five hundred miles of track were built during the conflict, mostly in the mid-Atlantic states.

The cost of the Civil War? Measured by the proportion of casualties to those who fought, the Civil War took the greatest toll of all American wars. The Union dead numbered some 36,000; the wounded, 275,000. For the Confederates it was 258,000 dead and 100,000 wounded.

Now that 4 million slaves had been freed, what would be their place in the reconstructed Union? Congress passed three constitutional amendments that changed their status. The Thirteenth Amendment abolished slavery throughout the United States. The Fourteenth Amendment asserted the equal citizenship of all blacks. And the Fifteenth Amendment assured the vote for all male citizens regardless of race or color.

This is not the place to go into what happened afterward. It is enough here to say that too many problems were left unsolved in the plans for rebuilding the South. And there were just not enough people, northern as well as southern, who cared deeply enough about justice for African Americans. Yet the Civil War did restore the Union, it did free the slaves, and it did enable black people to organize and to fight for a better life for all who suffer from injustice and inequality.

Chapter 7

BUILDING THE TRANSCONTINENTAL

EVEN AS THE FURY OF THE CIVIL WAR MOUNTED, PRESIDENT
Lincoln and Congress took the first steps toward building a transcontinental
railroad. In 1862, Congress passed the Pacific Railroad Act. The bill states that
the railway was to be built by two companies: the Union Pacific to build
westward from the Missouri River, and the Central Pacific to build eastward
from Sacramento, California. It would be a cooperative project between government and private enterprise.

The driving force behind the project for many years was young Theodore
D. Judah, graduate of an engineering school. He had the support of Lincoln,
once the lawyer for the Rock Island Railroad, and four powerful California
merchants (the Big Four). Years of publicity, pamphleteering, lobbying,
speechifying, and bribery finally paid off.

Congress provided substantial land grants and financial aid for the project, and when that proved not enough, it gave still more help in 1864. It doubled the size of the railroads' land grants and offered other inducements in
order to attract investors. During the war years, Congress gave over 100 million acres to railroads, all free of charge. No wonder railroad stocks climbed
to unheard-of prices. The railroads became the country's first big business.

True, Congress also passed the Homestead Act, setting aside 160 acres of public lands in the West for each person who would cultivate it for five years. If you could afford to pay $1.25 an acre, you could acquire a homestead. But a city worker, making about $250 a year, couldn't raise the funds to file a claim, let alone raise the additional money needed to buy farm equipment and move to the West. Much of the Homestead land wound up in the hands of large companies at prices well below their actual value.

As the railroad corporations expanded, they needed more and more capital. Investment firms that helped provide the funding became closely connected to the railroads. The bankers wanted to stop the brazen fraud of the railroads and to create greater stability that would ensure high profits—but within the law. By the 1890s, the country's rail system was dominated by six huge lines, four of them controlled by banker J. P. Morgan. Half the nation's rail mileage was now in his hands.

The railroad lawyers preached the virtues of individualism and private property. "The great curse of the world," they proclaimed, "is too much government." (But not when that government was controlled by themselves. Samuel J. Tilden, for instance, a corporate lawyer with many railroad companies as his clients, was elected governor of New York, and then tried, unsuccessfully, to win the White House.)

When the Civil War ended, the railroads quickly moved beyond the old frontier. Their lines made possible extensive settlement, which led to admission of the new territories to the Union. In 1865 the West had only 960 miles of track. In the next fifty years, this soared to over ninety thousand miles.

The newcomers found a West vastly different from the territory settled east of the Mississippi. Land? Plenty of it, far more than dreamed of. But the "Great American Desert," as it was mistakenly called, was short of timber and water. The problem of meager rainfall and seasons of drought was met by the windmill, new dry-farming methods, and irrigation projects. Barbed wire substituted for wooden fencing and homes were built of sod instead of wood.

As for the vast distances, the railroads would take care of that, bringing in many settlers and opening up eastern markets for western farm products.

Building the new rail lines progressed in stages. Surveyors moved on ahead to map out the route and find the easiest grade for the roadbeds and supplies of water for the locomotives. Each surveying team consisted of an experienced engineer, two assistant engineers, rodmen, flagmen, and chain men, all recently graduated civil engineers without practical experience. The team of some twenty men were all armed to operate in hostile Indian country. Most had served in the Civil War.

Rails and equipment were sent out to the chosen sites,

ENGINEERS RESTING DURING A PRELIMINARY SURVEY FOR A TRANSCONTINENTAL RAILWAY LINE.

together with gangs of tracklayers, mostly Irish. Construction materials were piled up in the yards at Omaha and forwarded as needed. Company executives back in Boston and New York peppered the supervisors with urgent telegrams, demanding that more and more track be laid. New stretches of the line meant that the company could sell more bonds and acquire more land.

Most of the railroads had their goal set on reaching the Pacific Coast. Few lines ran north or south. With little traffic to count on in those early stages, the lines constantly sought funds to pay for construction. Towns, cities, and states, eager for tracks to be located close by, added their subsidies to the federal government's.

That first transcontinental railroad "was built with blood, sweat, politics and thievery," wrote historian Howard Zinn. The Union Pacific created a dummy company, called the Credit Mobilier, to do the construction work at a highly inflated rate for all expenses incurred. It paid the company $94 million for the job, when the actual cost was $44 million. The fat profits went into Union Pacific pockets. Shares in the Credit Mobilier were sold cheaply to congressmen, to gain their support and to forestall investigations. A director of the company, Congressman Oakes Ames, declared, "There is no difficulty in getting men to look after their own property."

When Congress investigated the Credit

CONGRESSMAN OAKES AMES (1804–1873).

WORKERS BUILDING THE UNION PACIFIC RAILROAD IN NEBRASKA.

Mobilier chicanery in the 1870s, Ames and other congressmen were ruined by the scandal.

By the end of 1866, a total of 293 miles of track had been laid from Omaha to a base construction camp at North Platte, Nebraska. Chief engineer for the Union Pacific was Grenville M. Dodge, a Union Army general. He ran the construction project as though it were an army, and he employed some ten thousand workers and almost as many draft animals.

Dodge assigned two brothers, Jack and Dan Casement, to get the track laid. They recruited Irish laborers, many of whom were veterans of the Civil War. Famine had caused a huge immigration of Irish to America between 1846

and 1854. Many of the Irish came penniless and with little education. Few had trades or industrial skills. They got jobs no one else wanted—cheap day labor such as building railroads or digging canals. Irish women worked mostly as domestic servants. Like the men, they worked long hours for low pay.

Life was made no easier by the widespread prejudice against the Irish. People scorned their nationality; ridiculed their faith; sneered at their customs, manners, and speech. They were barred from occupations and neighborhoods. Yet when the Civil War began, many Irishmen were among the foreign-born who volunteered or were drafted for service.

Now, taken on by the Union Pacific construction project, they were part of the work crews that followed the surveyors. The graders came first, moving millions of tons of earth from cuts through rises into fills over depressions. And then, with hand shovels, they shaped the roadbed, in one-hundred-mile segments.

Tracklayers followed. Five men lifted each 560-pound rail, pulling it on

THE GREAT MONEYMAKER

THE North wanted to end the South's rebellion quickly. But not everyone in the North! Historian Roy Meredith noted that "inside and outside the government there were those who welcomed the war as a means of getting rich, and hoped it would never end. The heyday of the war profiteer had arrived, and not a day went by on Wall Street without some new combination, a railroad promotion, or a new corner on the market." The great moneymaker of the age would be railroads.

President Lincoln was not blind to what was going on. "Every foul bird abroad and every dirty reptile up," he said in despair. Thieving war contractors and influence peddlers seemed to be everywhere. It was an age when fraud, bribery, slander, and guns, too, were normal aspects of competition. War contracts were let at 100 percent profit, diseased cattle were sold for soldiers' food, defective weapons and shoddy cloth for uniforms were manufactured. All without government inspection or penalty.

One of the greediest politicians of that time was Simon Cameron of Pennsylvania. In a political deal within the Republican machine, he was given the post of secretary of war in the president's Cabinet. Under his rule, corruption became rampant. To enrich himself and his political pals, he handed out war contracts, especially military transportation contracts favoring railroads in which he had financial interests. Despite the corruption, by the end of 1861, the North's railroads reached a high level of operation.

The construction of both the Central Pacific and the Union Pacific railroads is an example of the role of the big-time operators. Theodore Judah, the chief engineer, was interested in making a railroad. The Big Four managers of the railroad corporation—Leland Stanford, Mark Hopkins, Collis P. Huntington, and Charles Crocker, also known as the California Quartet—were interested in making money. They all became millionaires. They got their project off to an easy start by securing a loan of $1,659,000 from the state of California (governed by Stanford), and, by lying to President Lincoln, got a federal subsidy of $48,000 per mile instead of $16,000, which should have been the rate. Huntington, a tough lobbyist, misrepresented the length of the railroad and the terrain it occupied—a "normal" practice in that era. Historian Eric Hobsbawm holds that the Big Four "unblushingly" charged three times the actual cost of building the Central Pacific Railroad.

Men bearing the nickname "robber baron"—Jim Fisk, Jay Gould, Cornelius Vanderbilt, and others—bought up and looted existing railways as well as everything else they could lay their hands on. When Vanderbilt died in 1877, his fortune of $100 million led to the creation of a new term: "multi-millionaire."

Yet many of the robber barons, greedy though they were and crooked as the Credit Mobilier scandal proved some to be, did succeed in using their railroad empires to enhance the economic development of large areas of America.

WILLIAM HENRY VANDERBILT (1821–1885) SUCCEEDED CORNELIUS VANDERBILT AS HEAD OF THE NEW YORK CENTRAL. AN 1879 CARTOON DEPICTS HIM AS THE MODERN COLOSSUS MANIPULATING RAILROADS.

rollers into place. At the yell of "Down!" they dropped the rail into position. Then the gaugers adjusted the width of the rails, and spikers finished the job with three blows to each spike, ten spikes to the rail, four hundred rails per mile. They operated rapidly, laying four lengths of rail per minute. The result? Two thousand miles of track.

Neither a perfect job nor a guarantee of safety was the objective. Speed and minimum cost were what the bigwigs wanted.

All day long the Irish workers were ordered, "Mick, do this! Mick, do that!" And they shouted back, "The devil take the railroad!" They laid tracks to the beat of a work song:

> Then drill, my Paddies, drill—
> Drill, my heroes, drill,
> Drill all day, no sugar in your tay
> Workin' on the U.P. railway.

The rhythm of their labor carried over into their sleep. They continued to feel the vibrations of the sledgehammers in their hands and arms and the pounding ring in their heads:

> When I lay me down to sleep,
> The ugly bugs around me creep;
> Bad luck to the wink that I can sleep,
> While workin' on the railroad.

Eager to build as much subsidized track as possible, overseers insisted on hurrying the job with flimsy bridges, narrow embankments, and improperly ballasted track. Not only future passengers were endangered, but also the men on the job. Their accident rate was so high that it was commonly said, "There's an Irishman buried under every tie." Irish laborers, said one immigrant, are "thought nothing of more than *dogs*, despised and kicked about."

The Irish were exploited not only as laborers. Employers pitted them against workers of other groups—the Chinese and the African Americans. Competition between the Irish and the other groups was provoked, and it often climaxed in physical battles, on both the East and West Coasts. It was the old practice of divide and conquer. Its effect was to keep wages down.

Nevertheless, at great cost to labor and great profit to the Union Pacific, the track moved relentlessly west to its destined meeting with the Central Pacific Railroad.

WORKMEN ON THE UNION PACIFIC IN THE 1860s.

Chapter 8

A CHINESE MIRACLE

At THE FAR END OF THE CONTINENT, THOUSANDS OF CHINESE immigrants were hired by the Central Pacific to help lay tracks for the line leading east from Sacramento. The company president, Leland Stanford, praised the Chinese as "quiet, peaceable, industrious, economical—ready and apt to learn all the different kinds of work" that construction called for. When white workers hollered that whites should get all the jobs, Stanford told them they could quit if they liked, and he would hire nobody but the Chinese.

Charles Crocker, one of the California Quartet who ran the Central Pacific, took charge of the vast construction project. Within two years, he put twelve thousand Chinese to work, making up 90 percent of his labor force. The Central Pacific saved an enormous amount of money by doing so. It paid both white and Chinese workers a dollar a day, but whites got room and board on top of that, while the Chinese had to make do for themselves. The company thus cut costs by one-third.

The company made even more profit on the Chinese by also using them to do skilled labor—masonry, blacksmithing, explosives handling—at their usual rate. Whites with such skills were paid not a dollar a day, but three to five dollars a day.

CHINESE WORKERS CAMPED BESIDE THEIR CONSTRUCTION TRAIN IN NEVADA.

The Chinese lived in low cloth tents or in dugouts, and each gang brought along its own cook to prepare Chinese-style meals. The cook also had a large boiler of hot water ready each night when the men came off the job. They would sponge themselves down and change into clean clothes before eating.

In the fall of 1865, the Chinese crews began the attack on a huge mountain called Cape Horn. They had to build a graded, winding roadbed for the track against its side. They chopped and shoveled their way around the face of the massive granite wall. When there was no longer any surface for them to stand on, they were swung out into empty space by ropes suspended from the cliff high above. With hammers and hand drills, they made holes in the

Pushing eastward from California toward Utah, the Central Pacific's Chinese laborers bridged many of the High Sierra's chasms with timber trestles.

sheer rock, tamped in gunpowder, and set fuses. Hoisted out of danger, they fired the blast. With a great roar, tons of rock and earth tumbled down the slope. Foot by foot they notched out the narrow shelf, climbing some two thousand feet above the river tumbling below.

With painful slowness, the railhead was pushed on, past little mining towns with names like Gold Run, Red Dog, You Bet, and Little York. In the spring of 1866, above Dutch Flat, the heavy work of boring tunnels through Cape Horn Mountain began. It took five months to go the fifteen miles to Cisco, six thousand feet above sea level. With winter just ahead, workers faced deep gorges and thickly timbered ridges. Most of the tunneling was to be done in this stretch of terrain.

That winter the snow fell early. Storm after storm blew up—forty-four of them—making it the worst winter in many years. The Chinese worked in snow up to their knees, then to their waists, pausing only in howling gales.

Half the workforce, now ten thousand men, shoveled snow to bare the ground for the grading crews. When the snow overcame them, they moved into tunnel work. The rock rubble they made by drilling and blasting had to be

DIGGING OUT A RAILROAD IN COLORADO'S MOUNTAINS DURING HEAVY SNOW.

THE ENTRANCE TO A TUNNEL
UNDER CONSTRUCTION.

passed from hand to hand and piled in dumps outside the tunnels. In February a four-day blizzard roared in, stopping all work. Then, for five days, gale winds piled the snow into drifts sixty feet deep. For another five days, snow again, ten feet more of it falling. Locomotives were ganged up to push snowplows through drifts and to pull supply trains after them. When the trains stalled, regiments of Chinese snow shovelers had to dig them out.

With weather so bad, dugouts could not be made. The tents were feeble protection against the relentless weather, and the suffering and privation seemed endless. On the job, avalanches of snow were a constant threat. One reporter told of a snowslide that engulfed two

Chinese workers. "Seeing it approach, they stepped behind a tall rock, but it buried them 50 feet deep. In spring their bodies were found standing upright, with shovels in their hands."

There were greater disasters. Snowbanks massed on the crags above Donner Pass began to slide. Thousands of tons of earth and rock came smashing down without warning. A twenty-man Chinese crew was caught in the open near the entrance of Tunnel Number 9. It was the winter's worst killing; none survived. Again and again, Chinese workers were killed by blizzards and avalanches.

Three shifts of men working day and night pushed the tunnels through. The biggest of the tunnels, at the summit of the Sierra, was yet to be tackled. That winter, about eight thousand men began to hand-carve their way into Tunnel Number 6. When spring came, there were still fifteen feet of snow. As it began to melt, slides swept away bunkhouses, tents, and trestles. But the work went on. "The Chinese," wrote an engineer assigned to the tunneling, "were as steady, hardworking a set of men as could be found."

At the top of the Sierra, the granite proved to be harder than anyone had guessed. Cast-iron drills boring into it were blunted and broken. Gunpowder charges scarcely made a dent in the rock. The Chinese multiplied their charges but cleared only seven inches in a day. They labored in near darkness and foul air. "Conditions grew so bad no white man would have endured them," wrote one historian. Crocker was desperate to end the costly delay. He decided to try nitroglycerin. It had much greater blasting power than gunpowder, but it was unpredictable and therefore very dangerous. Nevertheless, he ordered the Chinese to try the explosive liquid in their drill holes.

The men cut and set their fuses, ran for shelter, and waited nervously. The first blast shook the earth, smashing the stubborn granite into bits and pieces. The trouble was, the men couldn't tell if all the nitroglycerin had exploded. The first worker to slam his pick into a patch of spilled nitroglycerin, said a reporter, "was disintegrated with a flash and a roar into fiery nothingness, and most of his fellows in the vicinity along with him." But Crocker went right on using the new explosive. Only when J. H. Strobridge, the construction boss, lost an eye to a flying chunk of granite did Crocker order the men to bury the nitroglycerin. They went back to using gunpowder.

A strange aspect of this story is that at that time, the steam drill had been developed to the point where it would have helped enormously. Crocker, of course, knew all about it. But he never used it, perhaps because it was cheaper to rely on Chinese labor, no matter what the cost to the laborers themselves. Never again were tunnel projects on that scale carried out by manual labor alone.

In June 1867, the Chinese rebelled against low pay and long hours. They dropped their picks and shovels and brought work in Tunnel Number 6 to a dead stop. They demanded a ten-dollar raise (to forty dollars a month) and a cut in the workday to ten hours in the open, or eight in the tunnels. What they wanted was fair and reasonable, but Crocker blamed the strike on "paid agitators" working secretly for his rival, the Union Pacific Railroad.

There was more behind the strike than wages and hours. The Chinese, wrote the *Sacramento Union*, were striking against "the right of the overseers of the company to either whip them or restrain them from leaving the road when they desired to seek other employment." Crocker was forcing people to work against their will, penning them up in detention camps, refusing them the right to change jobs, and using physical punishment to control them. Determined to do as he pleased, Crocker refused to compromise. He cut off shipments of the special food from China while the one-eyed

THE BIG FOUR

THE Big Four, they were called. Their partnership, formed in 1861, would change the map of America as no one before them had done. Leland Stanford (1824–1893) began as a grocer and rose to be the first Republican governor of California. Collis P. Huntington (1821–1900) and Mark Hopkins (1813–1878) were partners in a Sacramento hardware store. And the fourth, Charles Crocker (1822–1888), was a gold miner turned dry-goods merchant. With tiny investments, they got in on the ground floor of the fledgling Central Pacific Railroad.

Their goal at first was not to create a transcontinental railroad but simply to make fat profits out of building the first miles of track. Crocker headed the construction company and brought in the Chinese labor that added a new strain to America's ethnic mix. Stanford, president of the line, used his position as governor to promote the building of the Central Pacific. He did it by means that one historian said "would make even the sleaziest politicians today look like angels."

Huntington rose from poverty in Connecticut, quit school at fourteen, became a traveling salesman, then partnered with Hopkins in a hardware store. His assignment with the Central Pacific was to move east to handle financial and political matters. He lobbied hard in the halls of Congress, not hesitating to misrepresent the length of the railroad and the terrain it occupied. When the roads were finally joined at Promontory Point, Utah, Huntington set about assembling a coast-to-coast economic empire, operating in many fields, piling up vast wealth. Stanford, of course, gave his name to that university. And Mark Hopkins has the San Francisco hotel of his name to be remembered by.

ONE OF THE MANY BUILDINGS ON THE STANFORD UNIVERSITY CAMPUS IN CALIFORNIA.

Strobridge stomped about with a pick handle, threatening to beat up anyone who talked back. Crocker set a deadline for the men to return to work. If they didn't, they would be fined the cost of keeping their foremen and draft animals idle as long as the strike lasted.

What choice did they have? Alone in a friendless land, they had no union to back them up, and public opinion was hostile. Few whites in California had any liking for the Chinese immigrants. Work or starve, said the Central Pacific. The Chinese went back to their jobs.

When the last of the summit tunnels was completed, the railroad builders headed for the Nevada state line. It was the fall of 1867. The work crews were housed in old barns and sheds in the town of Truckee, California. A heavy snow came early, collapsing a barn and killing four men. The intense cold froze many workers to death. Before winter ended, the snowfall totaled forty feet. Still, in the harshest weather, the builders graded the roadbed beyond the state line, into Nevada.

To shield the tracks and to keep the road clear for work and traffic, snow-sheds and galleries of enormous strength were constructed. They were a series of timber tunnels fixed to the sides of the mountains so that avalanches of snow and ice could pass over them easily. The figures give some idea of the immense size of the task of building them. The project used 65 million feet of timber and nine hundred tons of bolts and spikes. The total length of the sheds and galleries was thirty-seven miles. The snowsheds built by the laborers stood the tests of winter superbly. Not one collapsed or was badly damaged.

The railroad kept moving on, down the east slope of the Sierra and out into the desert. From here on the workers would battle not snow and ice but sunbaked sand—five hundred miles of desert with only a few water holes all the way across Nevada into western Utah. Parts of the desert were so bad, said jokesters, that "even the jackrabbits carried canteens and haversacks."

The problem of obtaining supplies added to the hardships. The desert offered no wood, no coal, no food, and almost no water. Everything had to be brought in over long distances and difficult terrain. Thousands of Chinese climbed into wagons and, with tools and provisions, rolled out on the desert to prepare the grade for the tracklayers behind them. They began work at one spot in the morning, and by evening, equipment, tents, bunks, and offices were ten miles away at another site. Overnight, towns of five thousand inhabitants were created that by daybreak were deserted villages. A well-built roadbed stretched between morning and evening sites.

How the rails were laid is described by a historian of the Central Pacific:

> Iron trains were scheduled so that the first one each day pulled in and was unloaded at sunrise, while the work force breakfasted and was marshaled for the day's planned stint. The empty iron train backed into the clear. . . . Small flatcars were loaded with ties, rails, fastenings, and drawn by horses out to the end of the track. Ties were put down. The iron gangs laid down the rails while a Chinese distributed spikes, two to each tie; another distributed fishplates; a third the bolts and nuts to fasten them. Two to each side of the track came the spikers, nailing rails to ties. Two more men followed to adjust and tighten the fishplates, the flatcar rolling ahead in the meantime, the next pair of rails clanking down. Emptied at last, the car was tipped off the track to make way for a loaded one. [The Chinese] fetched the seven more ties needed to bring each rail length up to standard specifications and inserted them in place. Other [Chinese] spiked them fast. The boss checked and trued the rails.

WORKERS PAUSE FOR THE PHOTOGRAPHER COMMEMORATING CAMP VICTORY, UTAH, WHERE A RECORD-BREAKING TEN AND A HALF MILES OF TRACK WERE LAID IN A SINGLE DAY IN 1869.

By late November 1868, the railhead was nearing the Utah border. The outpost force of three thousand Chinese preparing the roadbed "had wrought a near-miracle," wrote a historian long after. They had succeeded in building a grade through a chain of canyons so deep, so gloomy, and so cramped that, it was said, "no man or animal ever had traversed it before. This magnificent grading job, done under the most primitive conditions and in almost complete silence and obscurity, stands today as one of the great engineering feats. . . ."

With winter came brutal, paralyzing cold. The temperature in northeastern Nevada could drop to fifty degrees below zero. The earth froze rock hard. The Chinese had to resort to gunpowder to blast it open.

By the spring of 1869, Crocker's crews were pushing across the salt flats of northwestern Utah, laying track at the fast pace of four miles a day. The end was near. The two lines, the Union Pacific and the Central Pacific, were racing to meet at Promontory Point, just above the Great Salt Lake. The grading gangs—Irish workers heading west and Chinese workers heading east—drew close. The Irish, resenting the Chinese competition, decided to terrorize the Chinese laborers. The Irish secretly placed a charge of blasting powder so that it blew up Chinese workers, killing them. Strobridge protested, but the Union Pacific ignored him. The Irish did it again. This time, the Chinese took their defense into their own hands. They planted a powder charge that killed several Irishmen and injured several more. That ended the unofficial war.

On May 10, 1869, the last tie was laid to complete the first transcontinental railroad. As the golden spike was rammed home, the news was telegraphed all over the country. The Irish and the Chinese were present at the ceremony at Promontory Point. When the official photograph was taken, however, the Chinese were forgotten.

They were left out of the photograph, those Chinese railroad men, but they did not vanish from history. They went on spinning the steel web that tied modern America together. It's hard to name a railroad line in the West or South that the Chinese did not build in whole or in part. From way up in

THE CELEBRATION AT PROMONTORY POINT, UTAH, ON MAY 10, 1869, WHERE THE CENTRAL PACIFIC AND UNION PACIFIC WERE JOINED TO FORM THE FIRST TRANSCONTINENTAL RAILROAD.

Alaska to deep down in Texas, they moved by the thousands, making the roadbeds, digging the tunnels, and laying the tracks of the Southern Pacific, the Northern Pacific, the Canadian Pacific, the Oregon Central, the Seattle and Walla Walla, the Atlantic and Pacific, the California Central and

California South, the Virginia and Truckee, the Eureka and Palisades, the Carson and Colorado, the Texas and Pacific, the Houston and Texas Central, the Alabama and Chattanooga. . . .

It is estimated that about twelve hundred Chinese—10 percent of the workforce—died while building the Central Pacific, and the bones of uncounted others are buried beside the tracks of many other lines. But who remembered them? Only ten years after the celebration at Promontory Point, novelist Robert Louis Stevenson (1850–1894) was traveling to California by train. He noticed a group of Chinese railroad men sitting segregated from the white passengers in a separate car. "Stupid ill-feeling," he wrote. The whites "seemed never to have looked at them, listened to them, or thought of them."

chapter 9

"THE INDIANS ARE IN OUR WAY"

To the indians, the onrushing railroads were the "bad medicine wagons." They were the latest in a long series of threats to their freedom that had begun in colonial times.

To the whites, the railroads were civilization pressing forward. Most white Americans throughout the nineteenth century believed that the Indians must give way before the westward advance of civilization. How could a way of life that whites thought "inferior," "backward," and "primitive" compete with their superior way of life? Whites wanted to farm the Great Plains, mine the mountains beyond, build towns and cities, and connect it all with a network of railroads. There would be no room for the thundering herds of buffalo or the tribes roaming the landscape in pursuit of them.

The whites meant to claim the land for their own use and profit. It was real estate to them, pieces of private property to be bought or sold as they saw fit. But the Native Americans looked upon the earth as the Creator's gift to all. They could not grasp what they would be up against. Boundaries? Private ownership? Such concepts meant nothing to them.

So when the railroads began to move west, stretching across the seemingly endless plains, they became the unstoppable engines of destruction for

THIS CARICATURE FROM AROUND 1886 DEPICTS THE CHEROKEE NATION AS BOUND, GAGGED, AND MUTILATED BY THE RAILROAD COMPANIES, THE U.S. COURTS, AND GOVERNMENT OFFICIALS.

the Indians. Trains bringing white settlers into Indian homelands created markets for a business culture totally strange to the Native Americans. The railroad also gave the invaders' military forces a rapid mobility that allowed the troops to bring overwhelming firepower against any resisting tribesmen. A nomadic people whose economy was based on hunting and the careful use of resources found it could not coexist peacefully with an all-consuming capitalism driving to expand.

Between 1865 and 1895, the U.S. government used bullets and bayonets to take land and exterminate Indians in more than nine hundred military engagements.

The Plains Indians saw from the start that the railroads threatened their existence. The warriors made raids on the surveying and the construction gangs. They cut telegraph wires, derailed trains, tore up tracks, and attacked and burned whatever the whites had. The railroad companies appealed to the government, which sent in cavalry and infantry units. "Until the Indians are exterminated," said the railroad surveyor James A. Evans, "no safety will be found."

The politicians held the same belief. "We do not let the Indian stand in the way of civilization," said former New York governor Horatio Seymour. "Today we are dividing the lands of the native Indians into cities, counties and townships. We are driving off from their property the game upon which they live, by railroads. We tell them plainly, they must give up their homes and property, and live upon corners of their own territories, because they are in the way of our civilization." And then, with the arrogance of the worst white supremacist, he added, "Theirs is a form of barbarism which has no right to be here."

The U.S. military, aided by professional hunters, set out to exterminate the huge buffalo herds in order to weaken the Plains Indians. Hunters were hired by the railroads to provide buffalo meat for the construction crews. One skilled rifleman could kill 150 animals in one day. The speed of slaughter was incredible, intensified by a profit motive.

For there was a great demand by the whites for buffalo robes and hats. In the early 1870s, eastern tanneries found that buffalo hides could be made into commercial leather such as belts to drive steam-powered factories. In one year alone, the railroads hauled 1.25 million hides from the plains. Many set-

SHOOTING BUFFALO ON THE LINE OF THE KANSAS PACIFIC RAILROAD.

tlers helped pay their homestead mortgages by selling buffalo hides and bones for shipment east, where they would be processed into carbon or fertilizer.

Before the whites arrived, it's estimated that about 75 million buffalo roamed the plains. By 1900 the number had dropped to about one thousand.

For the Plains Indians, all this meant the loss of their major source of food and shelter.

Did anyone in power care?

Chapter 10

MODERN AMERICA IS BORN

With the completion of the first transcontinental line in 1869, the railroads gained even greater importance in national life. They underlay every new development—in economics, in politics, in culture—in the last decades of the nineteenth century.

In the West (as before in the East), it became cheaper and easier to send foods to market and, in turn, bring in settlers, farm implements, lecturers, and entertainment. Competition became fierce for the privilege of becoming a regular station on the line. Rail connections to the rising new cities became so important that towns were made or ruined by the decisions of the big railroads.

"The big city of modern times," wrote historian Marshall B. Davidson, "was in large part the creation of railroads. Until they could throw out such lifelines into the food-producing hinterlands, and until they had speedy lanes of distribution for the products of their industry, vast, modern cities could not develop. Wherever rails were laid, old cities flourished with new vigor, others sprang into being out of little or nothing."

The cattle ranchers of Texas were among the boldest exploiters of the new transport system. When the Indians were forced off their lands and the buffalo they depended on were exterminated, the Great Plains, with their deep, rich grass, were opened up to grazing by cattle. Soon there were huge herds of longhorns, handled by cowboys whose methods were borrowed from the Mexicans.

With cattle fetching high prices, Chicago became the chief slaughter-house. The packers dominated the meat industry through the invention of the refrigerator car—simply an icebox on wheels. Armour and Swift, origi-nally butchers from the East, and one or two others monopolized the busi-ness by ruthless methods few questioned at the time. When the railroads at first refused to supply refrigerated cars, the packers built their own and then forced the railroads to carry the cars at prices the packers set. Additionally, the packers demanded that only their own cars be set on the line. So all fruits and vegetables shipped from anywhere in the country had to move on the monopoly's cars.

The long cattle drives—fifteen hundred miles from Texas—brought the cattle to the railhead at Abilene, Kansas. The Chisholm Trail, as it was called, became legendary in cowboy stories and later in movies and TV serials.

In many other ways, the railroads had a crucial impact on the economy. Great numbers of workmen were mobilized to survey the course of the lines, lay the roadbed and the rails, and maintain them. A single railroad company might have as many as thirty-five thousand employees.

But beyond creating jobs within the company, the railroad's needs called for mustering far more workers and materials. Rails had to be manufactured out of steel. Engines, freight cars, and passenger cars had to be built and main-tained in engineering workshops. Coal to heat engine boilers had to be dug out of the mines and shipped.

The needs of the new system of rail transport generated hundreds of thousands of new jobs, new mines, new steel mills, new towns, new markets,

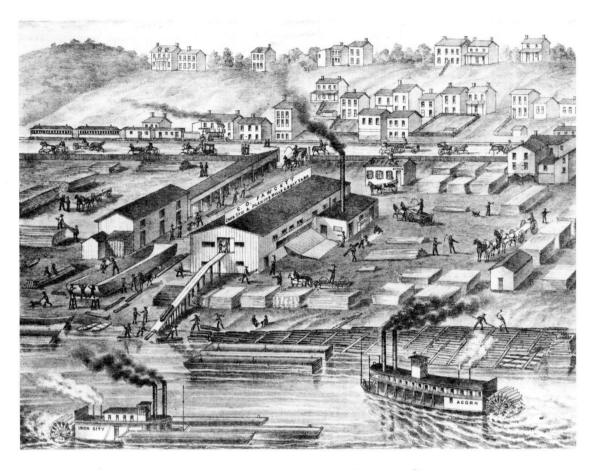

STEEL MILLS ALONG THE MONONGAHELA RIVER IN PITTSBURGH.

new skills, and new forms of financial and industrial organization. Historian Hugh Brogan summed up the influence of the railroad:

> It was this which began to turn the Americans into a nation of town-dwellers; it was this which, by the demands it created, stimulated the amazing growth in production and wealth that, before the end of the century, had entirely outstripped anything the Old World could show; it was this which began

an entirely new class structure; it was this which finally freed the United States from its dependence on overseas trade by generating a self-sustaining, continental economy. And so modern America was born.

But the railroad's influence ran beyond America's economy. It also played a role in reshaping world agriculture. Investment in railroads opened virgin land not only in the American West, but in Canada, Australia, and Argentina, too. For the first time, agricultural markets became worldwide. Not altogether a good thing, for it led to overproduction of food products—not more than people needed, but more than many could afford to buy. The result was a global agricultural depression from 1873 to 1896. That chain of events, plus bad harvest years and political oppression, account in part for the migration of rural Europeans to the cities—and for the steady rise in immigration to America, where millions hoped to find a better life.

The reach of the railroad network into all corners of the country was a great leap forward. Yet the lines needed to do more for better integration and operating efficiency. For decades both freight and passenger trains suffered from two devices that kept service slow and dangerous. To connect one car with another, a link-and-pin coupler was used. The brakeman had to stand between the cars so he could slide the link into the socket and drop the pin to hold the cars together. You could tell a veteran brakeman by his missing finger or crippled hand. An even worse part of the job was the manual braking of the cars to slow or stop them. The brakeman had to balance himself on top of the onrushing cars to twist the hand brake. Imagine how hard and risky it was to do this, especially during an icy blizzard.

Many inventors worked on the problems. Eli Janney (1831–1912) invented the first effective automatic coupler and got the Pennsylvania Railroad to be the first to use it. The problem of braking was solved in 1869 when George

Westinghouse (1846–1914) designed brakes powered by air pressure carried by hoses from pumps on the engine. It was not until 1893, however, that air brakes were made mandatory safety equipment on all trains. Within a year, employee accident rates dropped by 60 percent. And passenger accident rates went down to almost zero.

Still, railway managers were slow to adopt the new devices. Why worry about workers losing life and limb when labor was so cheap? It took years of relentless pressure by Lorenzo S. Coffin (1823–1915), a former teacher and Civil War chaplain, before laws were adopted requiring all trains to use both automatic couplers and air brakes.

Dozens of disasters built up public pressure for government regulation and inspection. The railroads, a private enterprise, served a public interest in the safety of transport. Why shouldn't the government step in to guarantee the protection of its citizens? It did, and it

A BRAKEMAN BALANCING ON TOP OF A
RAILROAD CAR DURING A BLIZZARD.

brought happy results. Passenger safety increased threefold between 1890 and 1914. By the time World War I began, there was far less than one death for each 100 million passenger-miles of service.

The last decade of the century saw two other important changes in the rail system. Track gauges of different widths had long been a handicap to efficient operation. Not until the 1890s was an efficient standard gauge required by the American Railway Association. Another, almost laughable, handicap was the crazy-quilt pattern of dozens of times based on several mean local sun times. For instance, when it was noon in Chicago, it was 11:27 a.m. in Omaha, 11:50 in St. Louis, 12:09 p.m. in Louisville, 12:17 in Toledo, and 12:31 in Pittsburgh. Train stations in various cities showed dozens of clocks, each with different railroad times. Think how confused the poor passengers were! Back in 1870, a railroad trade journal had urged the adoption of a single standard time zone system for the whole nation.

Finally, at an 1884 meeting in Washington called by President Chester A. Arthur and attended by nineteen nations, standard time was agreed on. The Prime Meridian at Greenwich, England; the International Date Line; and the division of the world into twenty-four time zones were established. The U.S. railroads set up four time zones—Eastern, Central, Mountain, and Pacific— for their operations.

Even before the Civil War, it was apparent that a better way of signaling and controlling train movements was needed. Step by step over the years, improvements were made. In 1922 a government agency ordered that certain rail lines had to use systems of automatic control. With centralized traffic control, a single person at a central desk could manage switches, signals, and train movements over an entire railroad division.

But what about the power needed to move the longer and heavier trains that were coming into use? Many improvements were introduced during the

"TO A LOCOMOTIVE IN WINTER"

AMERICAN poet Walt Whitman (1819–1892) welcomed the dazzling technological advances made in the decades after the Civil War. He believed the breakthroughs in science and invention would knit the world together. The Suez Canal opened, the Atlantic cable beneath the ocean linked Europe with America, and the railroad spanned the North American continent. "These modern wonders," he said, "will make possible an age of universal peace and brotherhood." In 1876 he wrote a poem delighting in the look and feel and sound of a train roaring through a winter storm.

WINTER TRAIN.

"TO A LOCOMOTIVE IN WINTER"

Thee for my recitative,
Thee in the driving storm even as now, the snow, the winter-day declining,
Thee in thy panoply, thy measur'd dual throbbing and thy beat convulsive,
Thy black cylindric body, golden brass and silvery steel,
Thy ponderous side-bars, parallel and connecting rods, gyrating,
    shuttling at thy sides,
Thy metrical, now swelling pant and roar, now tapering in the distance,
Thy great protruding head-light fix'd in front,
Thy long, pale, floating vapor-pennants, tinged with delicate purple,
The dense and murky clouds out-belching from thy smoke-stack,
Thy knitted frame, thy springs and valves, the tremulous twinkle of thy wheels,
Thy train of cars behind, obedient, merrily following,
Through gale or calm, now swift, now slack, yet steadily careering;
Type of the modern—emblem of motion and power—pulse of the continent,
For once come serve the Muse and merge in verse, even as here I see thee,
With storm and buffeting gusts of wind and falling snow,
By day thy warning ringing bell to sound its notes,
By night thy silent signal lamps to swing.
Fierce-throated beauty!
Roll through my chant with all thy lawless music,
    thy swinging lamps at night,
Thy madly-whistled laughter, echoing, rumbling like an earthquake, rousing all,
Law of thyself complete, thine own track firmly holding,
(No sweetness debonair of tearful harp or glib piano thine,)
Thy trills of shrieks by rocks and hills return'd
Launch'd o'er the prairies wide, across the lakes,
To the free skies unpent and glad and strong.

Civil War and after. They included better locomotive wheels, steel fire boxes and boilers, steam injection, and the use of soft coal instead of hard wood for freight engines, among others.

The greatest change, however, was in the size of the locomotive. By 1890 those for passenger service weighed as much as fifty tons, and those for freight service, up to eighty tons. Freight equipment increased in both size and quality. Designs for special needs were applied. As the cattle business grew, feed bins and watering troughs were placed in the cars. In 1872 P. T. Barnum, the circus magnate, began to move his "Museum, Menagerie and Hippodrome" from town to town in sixty-five railway cars.

What about the passengers? Was anything done to ensure an easy, comfortable ride for them?

Chapter 11

PULLMAN, PINKERTON, AND THE JAMES BOYS

DESIGNER OF THE PULLMAN CAR.

THE EARLY RAILROAD COMPANIES showed little concern for passenger comfort. But the train crews did. Take the Beaver Valley line, a spur of a midwestern railroad. "When the conductor had a hungry baby on board, he would stop the train at the first nearby cow, get out and milk it, and then heat the bottle on one of the potbellied stoves that were in each car," wrote James Dickenson in his history of the High Plains. "The crews were also known to shoot rabbits for the passengers' lunch."

For a vast improvement in night rides aboard a train, much is owed to George Pullman (1831–1897). One of ten children in a working-class family in upstate New York, Pullman quit school at fourteen to help an older brother in a cabinetmaking business. In 1858, during a terribly uncomfortable ride between New York and Chicago, he thought, why not try to develop a really comfortable sleeping car?

The first car Pullman designed wasn't much of an improvement. Discouraged, he followed gold miners to Colorado, where he opened a general store. In four years, he piled up twenty thousand dollars and went back to Chicago to gamble it on another try at the sleeping car. He was thirty now. This time, he came up with a second model, the Pioneer. It had two tiers and a hinged upper berth as well as improved trucks with springs reinforced by cushions of rubber. The car was finished lavishly with hand-carved woodwork, plush carpets, and fine mirrors. It was a foot wider, and the new upper berth made the ceiling two and a half feet higher than any car then in use. These new dimensions meant that station platforms had to be narrowed and bridges raised. In 1865, when Lincoln was assassinated, his widow insisted that the government commandeer the most palatial car to carry the body of

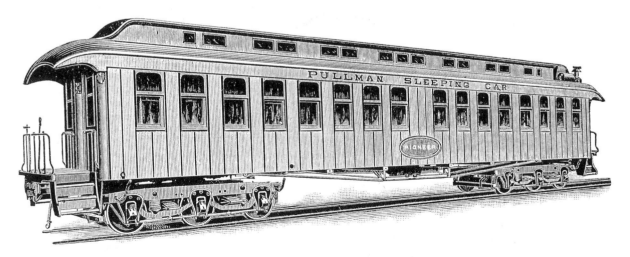

THE PIONEER, THE FIRST COMPLETE PULLMAN SLEEPING CAR.

the beloved president from Chicago to the burial site in Springfield, Illinois. Every line between the two stations had to alter its station platforms and bridges so the outsize funeral car could pass.

Publicity for Pullman's invention was enormous, and his rate of expansion furious. Two years after Pullman started, the Pullman Palace Car Company was incorporated and forty-eight of his cars were running on major rail lines. His second invention, a dining car, also proved a quick success. He saw to it that a Pullman car was on one of the first trains to make the transcontinental trip.

With Pullman's genius for publicity, within two years he was able to buy out or drive out competitors and gain almost a monopoly of sleeping car travel.

A GLIMPSE OF A LUXURIOUS PULLMAN CAR INTERIOR IN 1887.

81

While Pullman was making his car more luxurious, other passenger car equipment was being improved. Candles were replaced by kerosene lamps and, in the 1880s, by electricity. Stoves gave way to hot-water heaters. Steel gradually replaced elements made of iron until, in 1906, all-steel passenger cars entered regular service on the main lines.

Now the best trains offered conveniences and luxuries that most people did not enjoy in their own homes.

When dining cars became standard service, passengers had to cross swaying, open platforms to reach them. To secure safer movement, the Pullman company developed a flexible, covered passageway: the vestibule. Never one to miss a chance for even greater profits, Pullman built hundreds of private cars for corporate executives and other luminaries. These, of course, were the most elegant of all.

But elegance didn't guarantee safety. You could be tootling along happily in a train and suddenly be scared stiff when a

A FRENCH MAGAZINE OF 1905 FEATURES AN AMERICAN TRAIN ROBBERY ON THE COVER.

masked gunman rushed into your car and demanded your cash, your jewels, and your watch. In the last decades of the 1800s, that happened often.

Railways were first held up after the Civil War, when former soldiers trained to violence were prepared to get rich quick by train robbery. The Reno brothers and the Younger brothers formed gangs that preyed on trains in many states from the Dakotas to Tennessee. Romantic legends sprang up about the train robbers, portraying them as modern Robin Hoods: "merry men" who robbed the rich to help the poor.

This was far from the truth. The James brothers, Jesse and Frank, did not hesitate to wreck trains in order to rob them. Their train-wrecking career began in Iowa when they displaced a rail just as the train came roaring around a bend. The engine overturned, the engineer was killed, and the gang clambered aboard to sweep into sacks every removable item of value. They set a pattern that would cause the deaths of innocent men, women, and children, both crew and passengers.

Public opinion, surprisingly, was somewhat tolerant of the robbers. Farmers who felt cheated by high freight rates and investors who had lost in wildcat rail investments didn't worry if other men who needed money robbed the trains. Then, too, some people looked upon the train robberies as insignificant when compared with the greater sins of the big businessmen known as robber barons.

The thieves were helped by the lack of a national law enforcement agency that could cross state lines. If a train was held up in one state and the bandits disappeared into another, the local sheriffs had to drop the trail. Allan Pinkerton (1819–1884), a Scottish immigrant who had launched a private detective agency in 1850, saw a great opportunity in this. His operatives would cross state lines and track down the train robbers.

But when the Pinkertons went after Jesse and Frank James, they made an error that cost them much in popularity. They traced the brothers to their home in Missouri and tossed a huge firebomb through an open window. Jesse and Frank were not home at the time, but an innocent friend was killed and the James boys' mother had her arm and shoulder destroyed.

JESSE (LEFT) AND FRANK JAMES WITH THEIR MOTHER IN AN 1870 PHOTOGRAPH.

Neither the Pinkertons nor the police put down the James gang. Half the gang were killed or captured when their robbery of a Minnesota bank failed, though Jesse and Frank escaped. Jesse ended up shot dead by a gang member. And Frank? He "reformed" and pranced before the public in his own Wild West Show in the early 1900s.

The romantic view of the desperadoes made Western stories popular. Many dime novels about such characters won mass readership. Train robbers became the heroes of movies, too. Real-life outlaws like Jesse James, Billy the Kid, and Butch Cassidy touched something in Americans fascinated by shoot-outs.

But it was anonymous people, the men few reporters or novelists paid attention to, who were the real heroes.

Chapter 12

WITH PICK AND SHOVEL

J. P. MORGAN, BANKER AND FINANCIER (1837–1913).

THE CREATION IN THE NINETEENTH century of a long-distance railway network in the United States (and in many other parts of the world) was, wrote historian Eric Hobsbawm, "the most dazzling achievement of engineering known to human history" up to that time.

History books record the names of "great ones" of that era—investors and monopolists such as Huntington, Stanford, Morgan, Carnegie, and Harriman—who financed America's railroad construction. Though some investors merely bought up and looted existing railroads, others had grand, romantic concepts of binding the nation and the world together with iron rails and steam engines.

But who knows the names of the men who did the work with pick and shovel, crowbar and hammer? Who sings the praises of the anonymous ones whose labor and inventiveness made the railroad epic possible?

There were two main groups of workers: immigrants and African Americans. The immigrants came into America from Europe, Asia, and Mexico. Some brought crucial skills to the making of the trains and tracks. Most ended up doing the grueling construction work. The Irish, the Chinese, and to a lesser extent the Germans were the largest groups of immigrants to work on building the railroads, especially the transcontinental.

But there were others, too. Many African Americans, both slave and free, worked on railroad projects from the time the first tracks were laid. In the South, railroad companies employed slaves in both construction and mainte-nance work. They advertised for slaveowners to supply "a large number of able-bodied Negro men . . . to be employed in felling, cutting, and hewing tim-ber, and in forming the excavations and embankments upon the route of said railroad." Almost every railroad in the pre–Civil War South was built at least in part by bondsmen, said historian Kenneth M. Stampp.

In Georgia they built more than one thousand miles of roadbed. By the late 1850s, black labor was fast replacing white labor in constructing south-ern railroads. In most cases, southern companies did not own the slaves they employed. Instead, they recruited them by promising their owners generous compensation. The rail companies got most of their slave labor from the neighborhoods of their construction work, but sometimes they advertised widely in remote states when they feared a labor shortage.

The rail companies assured masters that the climate of the worksite was healthy and that they'd get back their hired-out slaves in good condition. This was a false promise, for employers of hired slaves had only a temporary interest in their welfare. Railway overseers could be as harsh as the worst

AN EIGHT-FOOT BRONZE STATUE OF JOHN HENRY SCULPTED BY CHARLES COOPER IN 1972. IT IS LOCATED ABOVE THE EAST PORTAL OF THE GREAT BEND TUNNEL, NEAR TALCOTT, WEST VIRGINIA.

plantation overseers, driving their workers so hard that they often broke down.

Blacks continued to help build the railroads after the Civil War ended slavery. Freedmen looked for construction and tracklaying jobs, which was better work than gang labor or sharecropping on plantations, and higher paying. Perhaps you know the story and song of one of their greatest folk heroes, John Henry. Likely born a slave in the 1830s or 1840s in Virginia or North Carolina, John Henry worked for a Chesapeake and Ohio Railroad contractor, like thousands of other freedmen after emancipation. His legend shows his commitment to undoing technology. The ballad celebrates how he met his death while working in the Great Bend Tunnel of the Chesapeake and Ohio sometime between 1870 and 1873. In building the line, engineers had to tunnel a mile and a quarter through Big Bend Mountain in Talcott, West Virginia. Nearly one thousand workers, mostly black, did the immensely difficult labor. John Henry was a steel driver, whose hammer blows drove the steel rod into the rocks to make holes for the blasting charges. When the rail

"JOHN HENRY"

JOHN Henry was a little bitty boy,
Sittin' on his mammy's knee;
Picked up a hammer and a little piece
    of steel,
"Lord, a hammer'll be the death of me,
Lord, a hammer'll be the death of me."

John Henry went upon the mountain,
Come down on the other side;
The mountain so tall, John Henry was
    so small,
Lord, he lay down his hammer and he
    cried,
He lay down his hammer and he
    cried.

That steam was on the right hand,
John Henry was on the left;
"Before your steam drill beats me
    down,
I'll hammer my fool self to death,
Lord, Lord, I'll hammer my fool self to
    death."

The captain says to John Henry,
"Believe my tunnel's fallin' in."
"Captain, you needn't not to worry,
It's just my hammer sucking wind,
Lord, Lord, just my hammer sucking
    wind."

"Look away over yonder, captain,
You can't see like me."
He hollered out in a low, lonesome
    cry,
"This hammer'll be the death of me,
Lord, this hammer'll be the death of
    me."

John Henry told his captain,
"Captain, you go to town,
Bring me back a twelve-pound
    hammer,
And I'll whip that steam drill down,
I'll whip that steam drill down."

For the man that invented that steam
    drill
Thought he was mighty fine;
John Henry sunk a fourteen foot of
    steel,
The steam drill only made nine,
The steam drill only made nine.

John Henry told his shaker,
"Shaker, you better pray;
For if I miss this six-foot steel,
Tomorrow'll be your buryin' day,
Lord, Lord, tomorrow'll be your
    buryin' day."

company decided to experiment with an automatic steam-driven drill, bragging it would do more work than any man, and at half the cost. John Henry rose to challenge the new drill in a contest. A wager of one hundred dollars was made as to who would win, the steam drill or John Henry. John Henry gave his all, beating the machine—but at the cost of his life.

Many men like John Henry lost their lives in such dangerous tunneling. Cave-ins, dust, lack of fresh air, falling rock, an inferno of heat, and premature dynamite blasts killed men almost daily. Around two hundred men died in the construction of the Great Bend Tunnel. In 1873, while digging the Hoosac Tunnel in Massachusetts, 136 workers died. Nationwide, the human cost was almost unbelievably high. Government records show that twenty-two thousand railroad workers were killed or injured in the year 1889.

After the Civil War, southern prisons became a major source for cheap labor on the railroads. Prisons were expensive to operate, and the states saw a way to make money by leasing out the inmates. Most prisoners in the South were black, many of them young—in their late teens or twenties. The railroads housed the men in work camps, under harsh and brutal conditions. Living in filthy shacks, fed poorly, and sweated to exhaustion, the convicts' death rate was as high as 11 percent. Penal labor on the railroads was little better than slavery.

A promising path to a decent future for some black men was opened up when the Pullman car was introduced. The porters were exclusively black, recruited at first primarily from the Carolinas and Georgia. There's a tradition that the first porters were drawn from former household slaves because they had been trained to "southern graciousness." Successful porters were asked by the Pullman Company to recommend applicants for openings, which is how many porters' sons, too, joined the company.

The Pullman Company became the single largest employer of black labor in the United States. In 1914 it had six thousand men on its payroll, and twice that number twenty years later. The job was valued because it might open the door to other, more advanced occupations and a better standard of living.

Porters traveled widely, saw more of the world than most middle-class whites did, met influential businessmen, and developed an outlook hard for a black man to come by in pre–civil rights America. Many African American men and women who rose to positions of power and affluence in recent decades have had fathers or grandfathers who worked for Pullman.

Until they organized their all-black union, however, porters got only a quarter to a third of the pay of white conductors who worked on the trains with them. Seniority did not matter to the company. Blacks could never expect pay raises or promotions

PULLMAN PORTER JOHN BAPTIST FORD IN 1924.
HE LECTURED ON HIS WORK EXPERIENCE TO
STUDENTS AT HARVARD AND PRINCETON.
HIS AVERAGE TIP WAS A QUARTER.

"THE GOSPEL TRAIN"

"MAKE a joyful noise unto the Lord," the Bible says, and gospel singers do just that. "The Gospel Train" and many other songs like it represent a form of folk music that developed in African American churches and soon reached ears other than the Lord's. The music originated in a deeply felt religious impulse, an outpouring of joyful emotion. In time, the richly varied experience of black people worked its way into the words and music. Just as anti-slavery poems voiced what fugitives felt on the Underground Railroad, so were the lives of black workers on the expanding railroads woven into "The Gospel Train."

"THE GOSPEL TRAIN"

The Gospel train is coming
I hear it just at hand
I hear the car wheel moving
And rumbling through the land

Chorus:
Get on board poor sinners
Get on board poor sinners
Get on board poor sinners
Get on board poor sinners
There's room for many more

I hear the bell and whistle
She's coming round the curve
She's playing all her steam and power
And straining every nerve

Oh see the engine banner

She's heaving now in sight
Her steam valves they are groaning
The pressure is so great

We soon shall reach the station
Oh how we then shall sing
With all the heavenly army
We'll make the welkin ring

We'll shout o'er all our sorrows
And sing forever more
With Christ and all His army
On that celestial shore

No signal for another train
To follow on the line
Oh sinner you're forever lost
If once you're left behind

Oh see the Gospel banner
She's fluttering in the breeze
She's sprinkled with the Savior's blood
But still she floats with ease

This is the Christians' banner
The motto new and old
"Salvation" and "repentance"
Are burnished there in gold

I think she'll make a little halt
And wood upon the line
And give you all a chance to go
But she'll make her time

She's nearing now the station
Oh sinner don't be vain
But come and get your ticket
And be ready for the train

The fare is cheap and all can go
The rich and poor are there
No second class on board the train
No difference in the fare

She's coming round the mountain
By the rivers and the lake
The Savior He's on board the train
Controlling steam and brake

This train has ne'er run off the track
She's pressed through every land
Millions and millions are on board
Oh come and join the band

There are Moses, Noah, Abraham
And all the Prophets too
Our friends in Christ are all on board
Oh what a heavenly crew

as reward for their long service. Their jobs could take them away from their families for weeks at a time. Tips might be good, though, if the prosperous white passengers were generous.

Early in the 1900s, about ten thousand Japanese immigrants found work in railroad construction. They were shuttled from one construction site to another. "We slept in freight cars," one of them recalled, "suffering a lot from the troops of bedbugs."

Mexican immigrants and Mexican Americans found work on the railroads of the Southwest. During the 1880s, they were a majority of the laborers laying track for the Texas and Mexican Railroad. Their pay was only $1.50 a day. With board costing $5.00 a week, there was little left to live on. By 1900 the Southern Pacific Railroad had forty-five hundred Mexican workers in California. They lived with their families in boxcars, shunted to wherever they were needed. The torrid heat of summer and the freezing cold of winter made life miserable. That was no concern of the company's. They'll work anywhere we want to put them, said the chief engineer of the Santa Fe line, and will do whatever we want. No wonder. Where else in a prejudiced society would brown-skinned people find jobs?

Still, during the 1920s, nearly half a million Mexicans, one-tenth of Mexico's population, headed north, across the border. Driven by economic desperation, they, too, became an important workforce in railroad construction.

Chapter 13

THE GREAT RAILWAY STRIKE

Hard times have occurred again and again in America, from the earliest days into the twenty-first century. The railroads were at the heart of one of the worst crises.

A depression began in the fall of 1873. It grew deeper and deeper until, by 1877, it engulfed nearly all but the rich.

It was brought on by many of the same causes that lie behind every depression. In their race for profits, businessmen poured money recklessly into mines, mills, and railroads. The furious pace of growth was forced by the craze for speculation. Eager to keep profits high, business overproduced in every market and squeezed workers' wages to the lowest possible level. Instead of sharing profits with their employees through higher wages and shorter hours, owners enriched themselves. Or they plowed profits back into still greater production. Millions of workers lacked the buying power the national economy needed to maintain prosperity.

After the first shock of that September, many thought that times would soon get better, but they only grew worse. Hundreds of thousands of men, women, and children were soon idle, many of them homeless and hungry. Year after year, the depression went on. By 1877 one out of five workers was jobless, and two out of five worked no more than half the year. That winter the count of unemployed stood at 3 million. Only a fifth of the workers were left with steady jobs. For them, wages were cut as much as 50 percent, often to as little as a dollar a day.

Railroad workers lost 30 to 40 percent of their pay. All in all, depressions would wrack the United States in almost half the years between 1873 and 1900. And they would continue into the twentieth century, with economic crises in 1907, 1919, 1929. . . .

Was there no union to protect the workers? Twenty years before, in 1853, an early union tested its strength. Railroad workers won a victory over the Baltimore and Ohio line. Collective bargaining between labor and management had spread to the leading trades, and workers struck more and more often to gain their demands. When a depression began in 1857, workers on the Erie Railroad walked out in the hope of preventing wage cuts.

But in the main, strikes failed. The labor movement did not make much progress during the 1850s. In the decades after the Civil War, few fields saw wages rise significantly. Skilled workers often lost their jobs to new labor-saving machines. The vast majority, semi-skilled or unskilled, suffered severely. In many companies, crews worked twelve hours a day, seven days a week. No wonder trade unions gradually arose to establish some balance in labor's bargaining position. They were needed to protect wages and to improve working conditions. Only the union could defend workmen against arbitrary treatment by either giant corporations or tyrannical foremen.

Why did it take so long, considering the conditions of that time, for unions to organize? Partly because of the strength of the employers and their grim determination to give nothing up. Partly because many native-born Americans still clung to the tradition of individualism. They felt that collective action by workers was wrong. Then, too, the ethnic and religious diversity of the labor force made it hard to coordinate a common effort. Unlike other industrial countries, America depended heavily on immigrant workers. Without shared cultural traditions and goals, conflicts and isolation from other workers clouded the common interest.

To make things worse, white railroaders banned blacks from membership in their brotherhoods until the late 1950s and 1960s. And firemen and brakemen tried to eliminate blacks from those positions. Nevertheless, many black railroad workers pioneered in organizing labor and in fighting for civil rights.

Another factor in slowing unionization was the belief of many workers in the success myth. They dreamed that they, too, would one day rise from the ranks to become self-employed. Those who took the lead in organizing unions were not trying to incite revolution. Mainly, the labor movement accepted both industrialization and capitalism. What workers asked for was simply a greater share of the benefits of the system. The unions that made up the railroad brotherhoods fought for "bread and butter" issues: higher wages, shorter working hours, and improved working conditions.

The great depression of the 1870s weakened or destroyed many of the trade unions. In 1877 the *New York Commercial and Financial Chronicle* assured its readers that "labor is under control for the first time since the war."

But the paper spoke too soon. That was to be the year of the most violent labor upheaval of the century: the Railway Strike of 1877, the first great collision between American capital and labor.

When the panic of 1873 broke, the railroads suffered like everything else. As the depression spiraled downward, roads went bankrupt. Profits could be kept up only by ruthless economy and cutthroat competition.

Wage rates were cut 35 percent in three years so that management could continue to squeeze out dividends of 8 to 10 percent. Grievances mounted among the workers. Lines of job seekers lengthened outside hiring offices.

JAY COOKE (1821–1905), AN AMERICAN FINANCIER WHOSE FAILED ATTEMPT TO BACK THE NORTHERN PACIFIC RAILWAY CONTRIBUTED TO THE PANIC OF 1873.

Those still on the job had to work fifteen to eighteen hours a day—and then wait three or even four months to collect earnings that were due monthly. On the Erie, trackmen who had traditionally squatted for free in shanties along the line were now forced to pay rent or get out. Some railroads even took away the passes the men needed to ride to and from their jobs. Sometimes they had to pay more to ride back to their homes than they had earned to run the train out. And living expenses in railroad-owned hotels away from home were so high that workers sometimes were left with as little as thirty-five cents for a day's work.

In May 1877, the Pennsylvania line put through a new 10 percent wage cut, and the men accepted it. On top of that, it ordered doubleheading, which meant one crew had to take out twice as many cars as before. So for even less pay, they did double the work—and saw half the other workers fired.

Then, on July 11, the Baltimore and Ohio announced a 10 percent cut, too, with unpredictably explosive consequences. The workers protested. Under a new scale, a fireman would get only $1.50 a day. How could he support a family and take care of his living expenses away from home on $6.00 a week?

But management was deaf to their protests. Quit if you like, they replied; we can always replace you.

And so they quit. On July 16, the day the new scale went into effect, forty firemen and brakemen refused to work. They were replaced, and the trains started to move. It wasn't the first time a tiny rebellion had flared and been stamped out. But this time, a great flame roared up as from an erupting volcano. At Martinsburg, West Virginia, trainmen seized the depot and declared that no freight would leave until their wage cut was restored.

The Baltimore and Ohio then insisted that the governor request federal troops from President Rutherford B. Hayes. Through his secretary of war, the president ordered four hundred soldiers to Martinsburg.

Meanwhile, trouble was racing along the tracks. At nearly every important rail center in the country, strikes broke out. At Pittsburgh on July 19, the Pennsylvania's trainmen took over the switches and the depot and refused to let freight trains move. The sheriff read the strikers the riot act, but the men stood firm. The governor sent in the county's militia—who promptly joined the strikers. When six hundred troops ordered up from Philadelphia arrived in Pittsburgh, they marched straight into a demonstration of men, women, and children. Stones were thrown, and the soldiers fired; twenty-six people were killed and many more were badly wounded. A grand jury inquiry called the shooting "an unauthorized, willful, and wanton killing . . . which the inquest can call by no other name but murder."

Strikes flared up in New York along the tracks of the Erie and the Central. The militia was called out, but it fraternized with the workers. Moving west, trouble broke out in Toledo, Columbus, Cincinnati, St. Louis, and Chicago. Everywhere, militias and federal troops aided by vigilantes fought strikers and rioters.

From the beginning of the uprising, most of the press had called it a

DURING THE 1877 BATTLE BETWEEN THOUSANDS OF STRIKING WORKERS AND THE MILITIA IN PITTSBURGH, THE UNION DEPOT AND HOTEL WERE BURNED.

communist conspiracy to overthrow the government by force and violence. The *New York Sun* called for "a diet of lead for the hungry strikers." It was echoing Tom Scott, head of the Pennsylvania Railroad, who advised giving the strikers "a rifle diet for a few days and see how they like that kind of bread."

In Chicago, the *Daily News* was able to look calmly into the background of the strike and declare:

For years the railroads of this country have been wholly run outside the United States Constitution. . . . They have charged what they pleased for fare and freight rates. They have corrupted the State and city legislatures. They have corrupted Congress employing for the purpose a lobby that dispensed bribes to the amount of millions and millions. . . . Their managers have been plundering the roads and speculating on their securities to their own enrichment. Finally, having found nothing more to get out of the stockholders . . . they have commenced raiding not only upon the general public but their own employees.

Judges might take the side of the railroad owners, but public feeling ran the other way. The *New York Tribune* noted that "the manifestations of public opinion are almost everywhere in sympathy with the insurrection." Sympathy with the strikers was the other face of hatred for the railroad corporations. Pittsburgh, where the citizens wrecked the railroad's property, was proof enough. The people had suffered from four terrible years of depression and they understood the railroad workers' grievances. They felt the same bitterness and discontent. They would not stand by and watch government troops offer bullets in place of bread. They demonstrated with the strikers and fought to defend them from the troops. A Scranton paper, the *Republican*, said, "The popular heart is sound. It is full of warnings to the corporations to adopt a wiser and kindlier policy in their dealings with their employees."

"I talked to all the strikers I could get my hands on," a Pennsylvania militiaman wrote home, "and I could find but one spirit and one purpose among them—that they were justified in resorting to any means to break down the power of corporations."

THE STATE MILITIA FIRES ON WORKERS IN PITTSBURGH DURING
THE GREAT RAILWAY STRIKE OF 1877.

By August 2, the national wave of strikes was over, crushed by police, vigilantes, and government troops. But in the two weeks it lasted, the workers
had stopped most of the traffic on two-thirds of the nation's seventy-five
thousand miles of track. The railroad men had come close to winning. Some

of the roads had canceled their wage cuts to forestall a strike. Others had quickly given in to the strikers' demands. But enough held out to exhaust the strength of a movement that had no funds and no central leadership. When the peak of the riots was past, the railroads brought in strikebreakers, and the ranks of the strikers crumbled. The workers' only hope had been to panic the managers into quick settlement. When that failed, it was the end.

It was the end of their jobs, too, for many strikers. The Burlington fired 131 men because they had struck, and many other railroads did the same. But the *New York Times* did not see the great strike itself as a failure:

> The workmen have here and there compelled compliance with their demands, and in other instances they have attracted popular attention to their grievances, real or alleged, to an extent that will render future indifference impossible. . . . The balance of gain is on the side of the workmen.

The nation's business leaders drew a lesson from the universality of the strike. *Iron Age* summed it up:

> One point is probably settled for the present at least; the reduction in the wages of labor has reached its lowest point. . . . It would be a bold step in a wrong direction to give notice of a decrease in wages.

The strike called a halt to industry's relentless wage cutting. Now managers knew their men had real grievances that must be listened to. Workers were not dirt or stone, but human beings with dignity and pride.

"I LIKE TO SEE IT"

ROMANTIC writers of the nineteenth century tended to believe that science and industry were enemies of the arts. The sound of a lark singing could inspire a poem. But the whistle of a locomotive? Emily Dickinson (1830–1886), a poet who lived her whole life in Amherst, Massachusetts, was open to radical changes in the world around her. With many others she shared the feeling that these strange locomotives were friendly, domesticated beasts.

"I LIKE TO SEE IT LAP THE MILES"

I like to see it lap the miles,
And lick the valleys up,
And stop to feed itself at tanks;
And then, prodigious, step

Around a pile of mountains,
And, supercilious, peer
In shanties by the sides of roads;
And then a quarry pare

To fit its sides, and crawl between,
Complaining all the while
In horrid, hooting stanza;
Then chase itself down hill

And neigh like Boanerges;
Then, punctual as a star,
Stop—docile and omnipotent—
At its own stable door.

EMILY DICKINSON

A MODEL TOWN?

In 1893 ANOTHER SHATTERING DEPRESSION BROKE OUT. AS IN THE depression of 1873, millions were soon unemployed, more than twelve thousand businesses failed, and several of the railroad companies plunged into bankruptcy. Armies of the jobless formed in several states, petitioning the government to do something to end the economic crisis. The spectacle of cold, hungry, and shabby men begging their government for help inspired both pity and terror in Americans.

In that hard winter of 1893–1894, George Pullman, the sleeping car magnate, slashed the wages of his employees. Most of his workers joined the newly formed American Railway Union (ARU), led by Eugene V. Debs. Instead of dozens of unions representing specific crafts, Debs urged workers, whether skilled or unskilled, to organize by industry. "United and acting together," he said, "your power is invincible." He succeeded in combining several of the separate railroad brotherhoods into the united ARU. The ARU sent a delegation to ask Pullman to reverse the wage cuts. He refused.

George Pullman, you will recall, was a self-made inventor who piled up millions through the manufacture and leasing of his luxury dining, sleeping, and club cars. He was proud of his assembly shops in St. Louis, Elmira,

Eugene V. Debs (1855–1926), leader of the American Railway Union and five-time presidential candidate of the Socialist Party.

Wilmington, Detroit, San Francisco, and especially his plant in Pullman, the model town created for him close to Chicago. In his "utopia" lived five thousand workers employed in his factories. With their families, they made up the town's twelve thousand residents. The cars they produced operated under contract on 125,000 miles of railroad, some three-fourths of the nation's total trackage.

All the town officials were appointed by the Pullman Corporation. The company dominated every aspect of its workers' lives. It owned everything in the town—land, plant, houses, tenements, hotel, stores, bank, school, library, church, and water and gas systems. As employer, George Pullman determined wages; as landlord, he fixed rents; as banker, he collected the savings.

Pullman knew how to make his business highly profitable. He ran his town to be profitable, too. He got water from Chicago for 4 cents but charged his workers 10 cents. And the gas for which he paid 33 cents, he priced at $2.25. No wonder one Pullman worker said,

> We are born in a Pullman house, fed from the Pullman shop, taught in the Pullman school, catechized in the Pullman church, and when we die we shall be buried in the Pullman cemetery and go to the Pullman hell.

Pullman business was good business, even into the depression that began in 1893. During all its twenty-six years, the company had paid its stockholders an annual dividend of 8 percent. And now, despite the national misery, the company not only paid the usual dividend but piled on top of it a surplus of over $4 million.

The profits grew fat, but not the workers. Reverend W. H. Carwardine, pastor of Pullman's church, reported:

> After deducting rent the men invariably had only from one to six dollars or so on which to live for two weeks. One man has a pay check in his possession of two cents after paying rent. He has never cashed it, preferring to keep it as a memento. He has it framed. Another I saw the other day, for seven cents. The man had worked as a skilled mechanic at ten hours a day for twelve days, and earned $9.07. He keeps a widowed mother, and pays the rent, the house being in his name. His half month's rent amounted to $9.00. The seven cents was his, but he never claimed it.

A VIEW OF GEORGE PULLMAN'S "MODEL" TOWN.

When the depression came on, Pullman chopped wages 25 to 40 percent. However, he kept the same rents and prices in the model town. Sinking deeper and deeper into debt during the depression's first bitter winter, the workers felt they had taken all they could. Debs's new American Railway Union encouraged them. Because Pullman ran a small railroad, his workers were eligible to join. To avoid company spies, the union organized secretly in nearby towns. In May 1894, they sent a committee to the company to ask that the wage cuts be reversed. The company pleaded poverty, adding that it was only keeping the plant going in order to give the men work.

Reluctantly, the men went back to work, assured first that the company would not fire any of the committee. But the next day, three of them were laid off. It was the spark that exploded the pent-up rage of years of humiliation. The men called a strike at once. Nearly four thousand of them had joined the American Railway Union, and they looked to Debs for help. He had advised them earlier to go slowly, because he knew better than anyone how young and weak and inexperienced the new union was.

Pullman promptly shut down the whole plant. His policy was to wait out the workers until starvation drove them back. In a few weeks, their families were suffering terribly.

Debs tried again and again to get arbitration of the dispute. The company would not listen. The American Railway Union then voted unanimously for a boycott to begin on June 26.

On that day, the switchmen detached Pullman cars from the trains. At once the men were fired. Then the other members of the American Railway Union walked off the job in protest. The boycott had become a strike. By the second day, 40,000 men had quit; two days later, 125,000 were out and twenty railroads were tied up. Soon nearly every train in the country was dead on its tracks.

WORKERS LIVING ON A CHICAGO DUMP DURING THE 1893 DEPRESSION AND 1894 PULLMAN STRIKE.

It was the most effective strike on this scale the country had ever seen.

The effectiveness of the industrial form of union was evident. Railroad workers all over America flocked to join. Section hands, switchmen, brakemen, roundhouse workers, firemen, engineers, even conductors signed up in ARU lodges, coming in by the thousands. Debs knew, however, that this was still a rookie union pitted against veteran union busters. For even before the boycott had begun, his industrial union had been facing a far stronger force than Pullman: the General Managers Association, a semisecret organization representing twenty-four of the nation's biggest railroads centering on Chicago. Theirs was a kind of industrial union of the railroad corporations, just as the American Railway Union was of the railroad workers. Now they stepped in to help Pullman.

The railroads knew the boycott was not aimed at them; it was aimed at Pullman. But they saw in the boycott a chance to destroy the new industrial union movement before it could take hold of American labor. As the boycott was about to begin, the association's chairman said, "We can handle the railway brotherhoods, but we cannot handle the American Railway Union. . . . We cannot handle Debs. We have got to wipe him out."

So the association took charge. From years of experience with strikes, Debs knew that if the union was to win, it had to keep the strike peaceful. He sent telegrams all over advising the unionists to stop no trains by force. They were simply to refuse to handle Pullmans.

The managers' first move was to bring in scabs. With millions made jobless by the depression, it wasn't hard to find strikebreakers.

The next step was to arrange for troops to be called out. The managers knew this would make the public think of the strike not as a labor-capital dispute, but as a labor-government battle. They went to the attorney general for help. He was Richard Olney, a railroad lawyer for many years and a board member of several lines. Olney worked out legal reasons for the courts to intervene. He said the railroads weren't just a private operation but a "public highway." If workers quit as a group on that highway, they were conspiring to obstruct commerce. Federal judges worked out a sweeping injunction against all strike activity. The injunction was a legal device to bar Debs and all members of the American Railway Union from interfering with the mails, with interstate commerce, or with the operations of the twenty-three railroads now involved in the strike.

The unions were bitter. Federal power was being employed to break the strike. Why wasn't it being used to get George Pullman to negotiate?

When a marshal read the injunction to a crowd gathered along the railroad tracks, he was hooted and his deputies were roughed up. By President Cleveland's order, federal troops marched into Chicago on July 4. Governor

FLAMING FREIGHT CARS LIT UP THE CHICAGO SKY WHEN THE MILITIA SHOT INTO CROWDS OF STRIKERS TRYING TO STOP THE MOVEMENT OF TRAINS.

John Peter Altgeld protested the move as unnecessary and unconstitutional. But a federal attorney swore in twenty-six hundred special deputies, selected, armed, and paid for by the railroads and called by the Chicago police "thugs, thieves and ex-convicts."

Now the violence the association hoped for began. Excited crowds flocked to the railway yards and open street fighting erupted. With fourteen thousand men under arms, the city was like a military camp. The militia shot into crowds trying to stop the movement of trains, and a score or more were killed. Flaming freight cars lit up the night skies. By July 6, 1894, the city was near hysteria. "MOB IS IN CONTROL," ran the headlines. "LAW IS TRAMPLED ON. . . . STRIKE IS NOW WAR."

Debs said again and again—and local officials backed him up—that it was hooligans, not strikers, who were rioting. But the press ignored his charges, calling him a drunkard and a dictator. Across the country, editorials began talking darkly of revolution.

With the armed power of the government and the court's injunction thrown against them, the strikers became discouraged. The boycott was near defeat. Debs had refused to obey the injunction, knowing it meant giving up the strike. While Pullman refused to arbitrate, the workers had no other way to defend their interests. A grand jury indicted Debs for conspiracy. Some seven hundred union leaders were arrested. Debs was thrown into jail for six months for violating the injunction.

The strike was broken.

The American Railway Union was smashed.

What scabs and soldiers could not do for the employers, the injunction had done.

The injunction was nothing new. But its use in the Pullman strike turned the injunction into a devastating weapon against labor. The Supreme Court's

WITH FOURTEEN THOUSAND FEDERAL TROOPS AND SPECIAL DEPUTIES MUSTERED TO BREAK THE 1894 PULLMAN STRIKE, MORE THAN TWENTY PEOPLE WERE SHOT DEAD AS CHICAGO NEARED HYSTERIA.

ruling on the Debs case meant that an employer didn't have to rely on violence to break a strike. He could simply claim that his sales would be hurt by strikes, picketing, or boycotts.

From then on, no sooner was a strike call sounded than it was followed in most cases by a state or federal court injunction.

For some time now, American workers had been learning that their government was not impartial in disputes between labor and capital. In the Pullman boycott, federal power was placed solidly on the side of the employers.

Did Pullman end labor's hopes of making gains through industrial unionism?

No, for the Debs union showed itself strong enough to match the network of railroads united against it. What defeated the union was not the corporations themselves, but their ability to muster the federal army and the court injunction on their side.

MARCH ON WASHINGTON

THE GREAT RAILROAD STRIKES OF 1877 AND 1894 DOMINATED THE headlines, but thousands of other strikes erupted in the late nineteenth century. Between 1881 and 1905, an incredible 36,757 strikes involving more than 6 million workers occurred.

Their labor had made possible America's rise to the proud position of world industrial leader. But except for the skilled workers, most laborers shared little of the material wealth created by industrialization. Some workers, usually native-born whites, managed to climb into the middle class. Most immigrant workers, however, were stuck in poorly paid, insecure jobs. If blacks were hired, it was only as heavy laborers at the lowest pay scale. On the railroads, black firemen might be used to shovel coal, but they were never promoted to the position of engineer.

As the twentieth century came on, big mergers sped up. The Census Bureau reported in 1900 that 185 huge corporations controlled 2,040 industrial plants—in steel, electric power, chemicals, and textiles. The railroads, prodded by the great banks, combined into seven great systems running two-thirds of the total national network of 225,000 miles.

Ordinary Americans found little satisfaction in all this technological progress and business growth. As industries and banks grew ever bigger and more powerful, working people found they had less and less to say about the way they lived. Forces beyond their control ran the show. The pay they earned and the prices they paid for goods were decided by corporate executives in remote offices or by the impersonal movements of world trade. The poor and the rich increased in number, as the gap between them kept widening.

With the nation's population doubling in each generation, railroad freight traffic exploded. Americans relied more and more on railroads for transport of every kind, while traffic on rivers, canals, and waterways declined. Several elaborate railway stations were built. The greatest of all were the Union Station in Washington, D.C., and the Pennsylvania and Grand Central Stations in New York City.

The great rise in rail traffic meant an increase in the number of jobs, too. By 1912, 2 million people, or one worker in every twenty-five, were employed on the railroads.

Pay at this time went up almost as fast as productivity. In the early 1900s, pay rises generally matched the increase in the cost of living. The operating staff did best. In 1908 engineers got $4.46 per day; conductors, $3.83; firemen, $2.76; and brakemen, $2.64.

The growth of railway unions had everything to do with the fairly high wage scales. With the industrial American Railway Union long gone, there were now twenty different railroad brotherhoods (as the rail unions were called).

By World War I (1914–1918), the railroads had expanded and developed faster than most parts of the industrial system. That growth helped meet the unprecedented needs of a war economy. Before the United States entered the war against Germany, it helped supply the Allies with products and equipment of many kinds.

INTERIOR OF THE OLD PENNSYLVANIA RAILROAD STATION IN NEW YORK CITY.

Rail transport was under such great pressure that a government agency was created to take over the lines. It operated them as a single system and succeeded in meeting the wartime needs. But twenty years later, during World War II (1939–1945), the rail lines tackled the massive job of wartime transport without much intervention by government.

Wartime emergencies often reveal the need for change. During World War I, the pressure on rail labor was so intense that the operating brotherhoods asked for an eight-hour day instead of the ten-hour day then in effect. When negotiations failed to get very far, the unions threatened a nationwide strike. The rail presidents would not give in, perhaps seeing the prospect of a general strike as a way of breaking the unions, as they had done twenty years earlier.

The rail workers countered by setting a date for the strike to begin. President Woodrow Wilson, fearing a crisis, got Congress to pass a law providing for the eight-hour day for rail workers. But the rail companies refused to obey the law, calling it unconstitutional. The union leaders responded by calling a strike for March 19, 1917. On that morning the companies gave in, and that afternoon the Supreme Court, by a five-to-four vote, upheld the eight-hour law.

The war not only enabled the rail unions to make gains in hours and wages, but it also gave African Americans a chance to find better jobs and a better way to live. When the war in Europe began in 1914, it cut off the vast tide of immigrants to America. Northern industries, straining to meet orders from the Allies overseas, were short of unskilled workers. Manufacturers sent agents south to recruit black workers. They promised higher wages and better living conditions. If migrants banded together, the railroads arranged cheaper fares. Some blacks rode free on passes supplied by the recruiters.

Trains pulled out of southern stations packed with blacks singing "Going into Canaan." As the trains roared northward, banners on their sides blazoned messages to blacks standing in the empty fields:

BOUND FOR THE PROMISED LAND!

BOUND FOR THE LAND OF HOPE!

FAREWELL—WE'RE GOOD AND GONE!

Migration soared. In 1917 and 1918 alone, half a million African Americans moved north. By 1920, a million had left the South to seek their vision of a Promised Land in the North. New York, Chicago, and Philadelphia now had the three largest black communities in the country. Other large African American centers took root in Detroit, Cleveland, St. Louis, Baltimore, and Washington, D.C.

Until 1914 blacks in the North had been shut out of almost all industrial jobs. They got the leftovers, the hard and dirty and low-paid work that whites didn't want. But the war gave them their first great chance. It produced big orders for industry. The blacks flowing up from the South found work in iron and steel and mining and auto plants, in the meatpacking and shipbuilding industries, and in railroad shops and yards.

The North held out hope of better jobs, better housing, and greater equality. But blacks did not escape racism. Some companies still refused to hire blacks. Others segregated them in particular plants. Usually blacks were placed in unskilled jobs, and generally they were paid less than whites were, though they received much more than they did in the South. They met discrimination in housing, were barred from white neighborhoods, and were forced into overcrowded ghettos.

Almost everywhere, white unions tended to deny membership to African Americans. Many of the unions within the American Federation of Labor barred or segregated blacks. At one time, before World War I, some 80 percent of the firemen on a large southern railroad were black. But within ten years of the war's end, only 10 percent of the firemen were black. Sometimes whites tried violently to drive blacks out of jobs. Such an open clash in 1932 on the Illinois Central Railroad ended with the deaths of ten black trainmen.

For many years, Asa Philip Randolph (1889–1979), an African American who as a youth left his home in Florida to settle in New York City, worked to organize blacks in his community. In 1925 a few Pullman porters asked him to help them establish the Brotherhood of Sleeping Car Porters. Prospects were dim, for the eleven thousand porters faced the grim resistance not only of the Pullman Company but of the federal government as well. It took many years of struggle for the union to build enough strength to face off with the company. Finally, in 1937, the company bargained with the union. It agreed to

A. PHILIP RANDOLPH,
LABOR AND CIVIL RIGHTS LEADER.

reduce the porters' monthly workload from 400 to 240 hours, and it provided substantial pay increases.

Later, when World War II began, Randolph organized a militant March on Washington movement to protest discrimination against black workers. The porters' union was the central force behind the campaign. Hundreds of meetings held in black churches, union halls, and community centers got over 100,000 black people committed to the march.

The first popular coalition of all sections of the black community, the movement forced President Roosevelt in 1941 to sign Executive Order 8802, barring the "discrimination in the employment of workers in defense industries because of race, creed, color or national origin." A Fair Employment Practices Committee was established to supervise the compliance of federal contractors with the executive order. In return, Randolph and the movement leaders called off the March on Washington.

Historians believe that Randolph's campaign was the real foundation for the civil rights movement of the 1950s and 1960s. The principle of equal opportunity for black people in employment was, for the first time, considered a civil right. The strategy Randolph advocated, of huge nonviolent demonstrations in public places of all kinds—learned from Mahatma Gandhi's successful policy in India and carried on by Martin Luther King, Jr., in the years ahead—helped pave the path to blacks gaining full equality.

Chapter 16

NEW TECHNOLOGY

IT WAS THE AUTOMOBILE AND THE AIRPLANE THAT RADICALLY changed the future of the railroad. Highways for travel by car, bus, or truck were built all across America, heavily subsidized by the federal government. Richly funded lobbyists for the giant auto manufacturers easily won the support of Congress for the Interstate Highway Act of 1956. The federal government was committed to spending $35.5 billion over fourteen years to build a national network of motorways. That law, wrote historian Hugh Brogan,

> was to do more to shape the lives of the American people than any other law. . . . It enforced the ascendancy of the private car over all other forms of passenger transport; it made continental bus services fully competitive with the already declining railroads; it boosted freight carrying by truck; it gave a greater impetus to black emigration from the South, and a huge boost to the automobile, engineering, and building industries, thus helping to stimulate the prosperity of the sixties; by encouraging car ownership it encouraged car utilization, thus stimulating the spread of the population into vast sprawling suburbs where only the car could get you to work, to the shops, to

schools, entertainments and voting booths; and this change in turn would soon be reflected in political behavior. . . .

Under such competition, passenger service became less and less profitable for railroads, if it ever had been. Some studies, as noted before, suggest that the real money always had been in freight. Still, although the railroads offered special incentives to draw more passengers, the number of riders dropped steadily.

Passenger service ended on thousands of miles of rail network. Many lines provided no passenger service at all by 1970. Travelers preferred to drive or fly. To reduce staff and expenses, some railroads merged. The biggest merger brought together the New York Central and the Pennsylvania, creating the Penn Central. But so many things went wrong that the company had to declare bankruptcy, one of the biggest business failures in U.S. history. Such failures were behind the huge shutdown in service, from twenty thousand intercity trains operating in 1929 to only five hundred in 1970.

Reacting to these facts, the federal government in 1971 opened a twenty-one-thousand-mile passenger service network called Amtrak—a contraction of two words: "America" and "track." Amtrak ran its trains over the rails of some twenty railroads, paying for maintenance and other services in long-term contracts.

As for Penn Central and other bankrupted lines, the federal government reorganized them into a new regional freight system, set up to make profits, and called it Conrail.

An interesting feature introduced around this time was the unit train— "one car repeated many times." Using high-speed loading and unloading equipment, one-hundred-car unit trains carried coal from the western mining region to eastern markets. Other products, too—such as grain, iron ore, and chemicals—moved on unit trains.

A TUG-OF-WAR TEAM TESTS THE LIGHTNESS OF THE ZEPHYR,
A DIESEL-POWERED, STREAMLINED TRAIN, IN PHILADELPHIA IN 1934.

An earlier innovation called piggyback service was revitalized now in the railroads' effort to increase freight service. Vans or containers of products were placed on flatcars for shipment, and service was speeded up by high-speed loading and unloading equipment.

Inventive minds saw ways to improve tracks and ties in that time of great pressure for savings. The new rails installed were continuous welded rail, produced in lengths of fifteen hundred feet or more, that cut out the old *clickety-clack* and saved a thousand dollars a mile per year in maintenance costs. While it once took an experienced section hand an hour to replace one tie, with new mechanical equipment, the same task now took one minute.

New technology began to revolutionize passenger traffic, too. The first diesel-powered locomotive was tried out in 1934 on the run from Denver to Chicago. (Seven years later, diesels were in common use in freight service.) Diesel trains could cross the continent without time-consuming engine changes. They cut twelve hours off the old steam-driven run. The benefit? A day saved for business or pleasure.

In 1930 air-conditioned passenger cars entered regular service.

Streamlined passenger trains—lightweight, lower, longer, and built for speed—cut down the time for long-distance schedules still more. For greater comfort, the old open-berth sleepers were dropped in favor of cars with private rooms. Slumber coaches provided tiny private sleeping compartments for only slightly more than the cost of a coach seat. Where runs passed through spectacular scenic regions, dome coaches were introduced. You could now see far more than from only the side windows.

In 1971, when Amtrak took over most of the nation's passenger routes, new double-decker superliners, so much more spacious, added to the pleasure of scenic travel.

One of the most used rail lines is the passage between New York City and Washington, D.C. Amtrak made it a high-speed electrified corridor, operating at 120 miles per hour. The tracks are jointless welded ribbon rail laid on spring-loaded concrete ties. All grade crossings were eliminated.

Sadly, however, what you sometimes see as you zip along does anything but gladden the heart. It is a landscape ruined by aggressive neglect. Decayed buildings, wild graffiti, junked cars, abandoned refrigerators, billboard advertisements, and garbage, garbage, garbage. Not everywhere, not always, but you wonder, can't something be done about it?

You wonder, too, about what the auto-based economy is doing to the country. Paved roads cover more and more of the good earth and defile the natural landscape. Exhaust pollution heats the atmosphere and darkens the skies. Trucks roar through city and suburb, shattering the quiet and endangering walkers. Should the federal government set stronger limits on these forms of pollution and offer greater support to the railroads for additions to routes in growing sections of the country?

Congress might consider this hard fact: Amtrak runs trains over the greatest mileage of any passenger railway in the world, yet it receives the smallest government funding for its operations budget. Trains pollute less than their competitors on the highway and in the air. Amtrak uses half the energy per passenger-mile that planes use, and a third less than cars and buses use, according to government studies. The new high-speed trains have an even greater fuel efficiency.

When it comes to land use, rail also has benefits. Trains take travelers closer to where they want to go. You get off right in the heart of downtown, instead of at a distant airport. And rail stations tie in well with bus and commuter-train stations and hubs. Rail can bring people, jobs, and businesses back to the central city, reversing the effects of suburban sprawl.

It was the motor and highway industries that brought about the decline of the railroads. They poured vast sums into lobbying for a national policy that placed one mode of travel above all others. Rail never got the same level of support as its competitors.

A look at other countries shows how effective modern rail can be. Travelers abroad enjoy rail service that is fast, frequent, reliable, and convenient to nearly any destination. If you visit any part of the European Union, you can find high-speed trains that zip you to your destination at speeds top-ping 180 miles an hour.

While in America the railroads struggle for government support, in other countries rail gets a fair share of government aid. Germany allots 21.7 percent of its total transportation spending on rail. France spends 20.7 percent. And the United States? It spends 0.4 percent.

Many legislators are beginning to pay more attention to backing rail transport. California and the Pacific Northwest may see high-speed service before too long, as will a nine-state midwestern network centered in Chicago, and areas through the South. Support is growing in Congress for a National Defense Rail Act that would do much to give the United States the kind of advanced rail transportation system it needs.

NELLIE BLY, WHO CIRCLED THE GLOBE IN SEVENTY-TWO DAYS, SIX HOURS, AND ELEVEN MINUTES IN 1889–1890.

Chapter 17

TRAVELS ABROAD

Railways started early in Europe, with Britain the pioneer. By the 1840s, lines had been built in many other countries, mostly short and unconnected. The first line built to link one country with another opened in 1843; it ran from Germany to Belgium and on into Holland.

By 1889 there were more than 220,000 miles of track in operation throughout the world. That year American journalist Nellie Bly made headlines by going around the world in less than eighty days using the global rail network. Without trains, the journey would have taken four times that long.

The clamor for more and more trackage continued. By 1900 rail mileage doubled again and electric power replaced steam as the driving force.

Here, taken from the historical record, are some sidelights on how railroads influenced life in various parts of the world.

RUSSIA

Russia is a huge country, about twice the size of today's United States. It stretches from the border of Poland in the west to the Pacific Ocean in the east. Getting from one place to another was difficult or almost impossible before the introduction of the railroad. The first tracks were laid the short distance from the Russian ruler's palace to the capital, St. Petersburg, in 1837. Later, the czar had the capital linked to the big city of Moscow. That construction was managed by Kleinmikhel, a military man known for getting things done—and notorious for killing his workers by driving them so hard.

A limitless supply of serf labor carried out the job. Serfdom had much in common with slavery, except that there was no color line. Russian serfs were white. Some noble landlords owned tens of thousands of serfs. The czar was especially interested in railways because he had been impressed by how rapidly an English railway had carried troops into Ireland to put down a rebellion.

The Russian government went on to plan other lines. Unlike in Britain and America, it avoided duplicating railways between any two points. Sometimes Russia accepted foreign investment in its railways. In 1867 it sold Alaska to the United States to raise money for more railways.

Building the Trans-Siberian Railway was the state enterprise that won worldwide attention. Siberia is a vast geographical region, rich in natural resources, that came under Russian control around 1600. Its nearly 3 million square miles cover the northern third of Asia. In many ways the project

WORKERS BUILDING THE TRANS-SIBERIAN RAILWAY IN 1895.

called for the vast energy and resourcefulness that put through America's transcontinental railroads. Work started in 1892, with construction carried on from both east and west at the same time. By 1902 you could travel from Paris to the city of Vladivostok on the far shore of Siberia.

The new rail line had a powerful economic effect. It transformed the life of half the huge continent, making possible an immense migration. Nearly 5 million people from all over Russia settled in new regions. Its social effect was vital, too. Russian peasants moving to Siberia intermarried for the first time with those from other ethnic groups.

The world fancied the railway for its passenger service. Its "International" train offered marble-tiled bathrooms and a grand piano for the round-the-world tours using the line. No one seemed to mind that the train's speed averaged only twenty miles per hour.

It's worth noting that the railwaymen's union in Russia was the most powerful labor organization. When it went on strike during the 1905 revolution, it prevented the czar from moving his troops and feeding the cities, placing the regime in mortal danger. Fearful of losing power, the czar made democratic concessions to his people to end the strike and to hang on to his throne. He lost it, however, in the communist revolution of 1917. In the chaos that followed, the rail system fell into ruins. It took a long time for the railways to be restored to working order.

BELGIUM'S KING LEOPOLD II (1835–1909).

THE AFRICAN CONGO

In the late nineteenth century, King Leopold II of Belgium decided he needed to build a railroad to improve the prospect of gaining maximum profit from his colony in the African Congo region. Without a transportation system, he could bring the territory's riches to the sea only on foot. In 1887 surveyors began to chart the route for a railway. The rocky landscape, the heat, the mosquitoes, and fever took a heavy toll. Not till three years later could the construction crews start to lay a track.

The line would be only 241 miles long, but it took up to sixty thousand workers three years just to build the first fourteen miles. They had to work through, over, and around piles of enormous stones. The whole route required 999 metal bridges, totaling over twelve miles in length. Leopold brought in workers from other territories in West Africa as well as from Asia. Among them were 540

Chinese, 300 of whom died on the job or fled into the bush.

The road was a terrible human disaster. Men died of accidents, dysentery, smallpox, beriberi, and malaria. They suffered from awful food and frequent floggings. Sometimes workers had no shelter to sleep in. If they tried to run away, they were marched to work in chains. It was said that "each railroad tie cost one African life." It took eight years before the first stumpy little steam engine hauled two cars up the narrow-gauge track that replaced the old caravan route.

In the 1920s, the French built a new railway through that part of the Congo they had seized as a colony. It cost the lives of twenty-thousand laborers, even more than had died building Leopold's railway.

PANAMA

It might be stretching it a bit to call a forty-eight-mile railroad the first transcontinental line, but the Panama Railroad was truly the first. The Isthmus of Panama connects Central and South America. Building the railroad across it looked like a good investment when U.S. settlers bound for Oregon and would-be miners fevered by the Gold Rush panted for a fast crossroad to the regions of their dreams. Now settlers and miners could take a ship along the East Coast to Panama, cross the isthmus by rail, and board another ship to sail up the Pacific to their destination.

It took five years to construct the short road that opened in 1855. It set a record for the number of workers it killed. At one point, one of every five men was dying every month. The laborers came from everywhere and were known only by their nicknames or as a number on a payroll. What to do about their bodies? Whom to notify? Who would identify the corpses in the morgue?

As a solution, says Panama historian Joseph Schott, the railway's doctor

THE ASPINWALL RAILWAY STATION IN PANAMA.

"pickled the bodies in large barrels, kept them for a decent interval to be claimed and then sold them in wholesale lots to medical schools all over the world. . . . The bodies brought high prices, and the profits from the sale of the cadavers made the railway hospital self-sustaining during the construction years." Later, the Panama Canal, built by the United States from 1904 to 1914, would connect the Atlantic with the Pacific by a waterway.

AN ARTIST IN 1881 PICTURES THE NEVER-FULFILLED SCHEME TO BUILD A RAILWAY THAT COULD CARRY SHIPS ACROSS THE ISTHMUS OF PANAMA.

A MARCH IN BEIJING IN 1966 TO SHOW SUPPORT FOR MAO ZEDONG'S CULTURAL REVOLUTION.

CHINA

During the Cultural Revolution, one of Mao Zedong's insane crusades, vast numbers of the Chinese people were relocated, downgraded, abused, humiliated, beaten, and even killed. Those who could no longer withstand the pressure turned to suicide. Paul Theroux, a writer traveling in China later, learned that people chose death by train rather than any other means. They would jump in front of an onrushing locomotive to end their torment. The reason? Buildings in the cities of that time were not tall. People couldn't kill themselves by jumping out of the window of a bungalow. And they couldn't afford to buy poison or a gun. Besides, if they were killed by a train, China Railways was obliged to bury them without charge.

INDIA

India, today the second most populous country in the world, came under British rule in 1757. (It did not win independence until 1947.) One of Britain's major efforts was to improve transportation by building railroads and

BEFORE CONSTRUCTION OF INDIA'S RAILWAYS, TROOPS MOVED ARTILLERY ON THE BACKS OF ELEPHANTS.

highways, partly for military reasons, partly because it was good business. Railways made it possible for troops to be rushed to any corner of the country where disturbances occurred. They also made it possible for English products to reach market everywhere and for Indian corn, cotton, tea, and other raw materials to be carried cheaply in bulk to the ports.

But the rail system also had unintended results. British business meant to keep India as an agricultural colony and a market for their industrial goods. Yet the very act of constructing a network of railways defeated that aim, for, inevitably, the railways required coal and iron, which meant an increase in industry to meet those demands. The railway system, as in the United States and elsewhere, became in India the forerunner of modern industry.

It did even more. Not only did the railway transform needs, but it transformed people. Says British historian A. L. Morton, "It created an industrial middle class, and an industrial working class. It bound the whole country into an economic unity it had never before possessed and gave it the beginnings of a political unity. It made possible for the first time a real struggle for national independence."

THE ORIENT EXPRESS

No train has been the scene of so many novels and movies as the Orient Express. Thrilling spy stories, bloody murders, glamorous romances—all have been imagined to take place on the luxurious journey from Paris to Vienna and Budapest and on to Constantinople (present-day Istanbul) on the Black Sea.

The first Orient Express departed in 1883. For quite a while it offered daily service from Paris to Vienna, but it went on from there into the Balkan countries only two times a week. It provided the quickest route to Constantinople for the many investors who hoped to make profitable deals with a sultan always in need of money.

Competition on the route began after World War I when other luxury expresses headed through Europe for Constantinople. By the 1970s, passenger demand was so thin that the trains were discontinued.

PASSENGERS DINE ON THE ORIENT EXPRESS IN 1884.

HITLER'S RAILROADS

Railroads are not thinking, feeling objects. They are mechanical devices for transport to be used by those who own or control them. During the dozen years (1933–1945) that Adolf Hitler was the dictator of Nazi Germany, trains were made to play a powerful and devastating role in the fate of many millions of people.

Trains carried Jews from the ghettos of the European cities where Hitler had imprisoned them to concentration camps where they were used as slave labor. The inmates were assigned at first to outdoor projects, including building rail lines. Not only the Jews, but others from all over the conquered territories of Europe, were conscripted for labor. They were herded into boxcars on long lines of freight trains. Without food, water, or sanitary facilities, they were shipped to Germany. They worked in factories, fields, and mines. Often they were beaten and starved and left to die for lack of food, clothing, and shelter. Industrial firms, short of manpower because of the war, drew on these prisoners for cheap labor.

But the trains were put to still another use. From Warsaw, Vienna, and Berlin, from Rotterdam, Paris, and Brussels, from Rome, Prague, Athens, Budapest, and Belgrade, Jews were deported by train to the killing centers of Poland until almost the last days of the war. At the Auschwitz death camp alone, 1.75 million Jews were murdered in less than two years.

It is hard to imagine the organization it took to accomplish that goal so swiftly. But the German railway system managed it. The dispatchers, the engineers, the track force, the signalmen, the brakemen—they were always willing to carry out orders. There seemed no lack of people ready to contribute to the Final Solution—Hitler's term for the extermination of the Jewish people.

Viktor Frankl, a Viennese physician, was among fifteen hundred Jews

THE RAILROAD TRACKS LEADING INTO THE AUSCHWITZ
DEATH CAMP IN POLAND.

traveling by train for several days and nights to an unknown station. They were told it was a munitions factory where they would do forced labor. Frankl heard the engine's whistle, sounding like a cry for help, and then, he said:

> The train shunted, obviously nearing a main station. Suddenly a cry broke from the ranks of the anxious passengers. "There is a sign, Auschwitz!" Everyone's heart missed a beat at that moment. Auschwitz—the very name stood for all that was horrible: gas chambers, crematoriums, massacres. Slowly, almost hesitatingly, the train moved on as if it wanted to spare its passengers the dreadful realization as long as possible: Auschwitz.
>
> With the progressive dawn, the outlines of an immense camp became visible; long stretches of several rows of barbed wire fences; watchtowers; searchlights; and long columns of ragged human figures, grey in the greyness of dawn, trekking along the straight desolate roads, to what destination we did not know. There were isolated shouts and whistles of command. We did not know their meaning. My imagination led me to see gallows with people dangling on them. I was horrified, but this was just as well, because step by step we had to become accustomed to a terrible and immense horror. . . .

Then the train moved into the station, and the doors to the freight cars were flung open. . . .

Now they were in hell.

GREAT BRITAIN

Britain has the honor of having introduced the world's first public railway.

Quakers put up the money to construct the Stockton & Darlington Railway. It was capable of carrying passengers, and it used steam locomotives as well as the horses that earlier were the exclusive power drawing the cars.

The S&D began operating in 1825, the year that John Quincy Adams was

THE OPENING IN 1825 OF THE FIRST RAILWAY LINE IN THE WORLD—THE STOCKTON & DARLINGTON. ITS PRIME AIM WAS TO HAUL COAL; PASSENGERS WERE SECONDARY.

inaugurated as the sixth president of the United States, that Beethoven's Ninth Symphony was first performed in England, and that a baseball club was organized in Rochester, New York.

The English saw the railway as the greatest visible force separating the world of their childhood from that of their old age. To Charles Dickens, the train was an avenging force, a monster ravaging all the green of the past. Novelist Anthony Trollope (1815–1882) blamed the railway for changing the appearance of London. He marveled at "the ubiquitous railway bridges and arches, which seem to return again and again, like the recurring horrors of a nightmare dream."

In the Dickens novel *Our Mutual Friend*, the railway is described as both creator and destroyer.

> Then, the train rattled among the housetops, and among the ragged sides of houses torn down to make room for it, and over the swarming streets, and under the fruitful earth, until it shot across the river, bursting over the quiet surface like a bombshell, and gone again as if it had exploded in the rush of smoke and steam and glare. A little more, and again it roared across the river, a great rocket.

To Dickens biographer Jack Lindsay, the railroad was the prime force wrecking the old England with all its vices and virtues, ruthlessly driving through into a new era. Dickens's feelings about it were mixed, contradictory. At times he hailed the railroad for its power to draw nations together in a goodwill that would end all wars. At other times, the railway became the emblem of the heartless forces of exploitation.

Bibliography

Ambrose, Stephen E. *Nothing Like It in the World: The Men Who Built the Transcontinental Railroad, 1863–1869.* New York: Simon & Schuster, 2000.

Arnesen, Eric. *Brotherhoods of Color: Black Railroad Workers and the Struggle for Equality.* Cambridge: Harvard University, 2001.

Bain, David Howard. *Empire Express.* New York: Penguin, 2000.

Bernal, J. D. *Science in History.* Cambridge: MIT, 1976.

Bobrick, Benson. *Labyrinths of Iron.* New York: Morrow, 1986.

Botkin, Benjamin A., and Alvin F. Harlow, eds. *A Treasury of Railroad Folklore.* New York: Crown, 1953.

Brogan, Hugh. *The Pelican History of the United States of America.* New York: Penguin, 1986.

Burlingame, Roger. *The American Conscience.* New York: Knopf, 1957.

Cahn, William. *A Pictorial History of American Labor.* New York: Crown, 1972.

Chandler, Alfred D., Jr. *The Railroads: The Nation's First Big Business.* New York: Harcourt, 1965.

Cole, Arthur C. *The Irrepressible Conflict: 1850–1865.* New York: Macmillan, 1934.

Daniels, Rudolph. *Trains Across the Continent.* Bloomington: Indiana University, 2000.

Davidson, Marshall B. *Life in America*, 2 vols. Cambridge: Houghton Mifflin, 1951.

Davies, Norman. *Europe: A History*. New York: Oxford, 1996.

Del Vecchio, Mike. *Railroads Across America*. Oscelo, Wisc.: Motorbooks International, 1998.

DeNovo, John A., ed. *The Gilded Age and After*. New York: Scribner, 1972.

Derrick, Peter. *Tunneling to the Future: The Story of the Great Subway Expansion That Saved New York*. New York: New York University, 2001.

Dickenson, James R. *Home on the Range: A Century on the High Plains*. Lawrence: University Press of Kansas, 1995.

Douglas, George H. *All Aboard! The Railroad in American Life*. New York: Smithmark, 1996.

Faith, Nicholas. *The World the Railways Made*. New York: Carroll & Graf, 1991.

Fink, Leon. *In Search of the Working Class*. Urbana: University of Illinois, 1994.

Foner, Eric. *The Story of American Freedom*. New York: Norton, 1998.

Foster, R. F. *Modern Ireland: 1600–1972*. New York: Penguin, 1989.

Franklin, John Hope, ed. *From Slavery to Freedom*. New York: Knopf, 1967.

Friedman, Lawrence Meir. *Crime and Punishment in American History*. New York: Basic, 1993.

Green, James. *Workers' Struggles, Past and Present*. Philadelphia: Temple University, 1983.

Haine, Edgar A. *Railroad Wrecks*. Cranbury, N.J.: Cornwall, 1994.

Hobsbawm, Eric. *The Age of Capital: 1848–1875*. New York: Vintage, 1996.

———. *Uncommon People*. New York: New Press, 1998.

Hochschild, Adam. *King Leopold's Ghost*. Boston: Houghton Mifflin, 1998.

Holland, Julian. *Trains: A Stunning Visual History of Railroads*. New York: Barnes & Noble, 1996.

Jensen, Oliver. *The American Heritage History of Railroads in America*. New York: American Heritage, 1975.

Jones, Jacqueline. *American Work: Four Centuries of Black and White Labor.* New York: Norton. 1998.

Josephson, Matthew. *The Politicos, 1865–1896.* New York: Harcourt Brace, 1938.

———. *Robber Barons: The Great American Capitalists.* New York: Harcourt Brace, 1934.

Kouwenhoven, John A. *Adventures of America, 1857–1900.* New York: Harper, 1938.

Landes, David S. *Revolution in Time: Clocks and the Making of the Modern World.* Cambridge: Harvard University, 2000.

———. *The Wealth and Poverty of Nations.* New York: Norton, 1998.

Larkin, Jack. *The Reshaping of Everyday Life, 1790–1840.* New York: Harper, 1988.

Levine, Robert. *A Geography of Time.* New York: Basic, 1997.

Licht, Walter. *Industrializing America: The Nineteenth Century.* Baltimore: Johns Hopkins University, 1995.

Lindsay, Jack. *Charles Dickens.* New York: Philosophical Library, 1950.

Lindsey, Almont. *Pullman Strike.* Chicago: University of Chicago, 1964.

McPherson, James M. *Ordeal by Fire: The Civil War and Reconstruction.* New York: Knopf, 1982.

Mencken, August. *The Railroad Passenger Car: An Illustrated History of the First Hundred Years.* Baltimore: Johns Hopkins University, 2000.

Meredith, Roy, and Arthur Meredith. *Mr. Lincoln's Military Railroads.* New York: Norton, 1979.

Milner, Clyde A. *The Oxford History of the American West.* New York: Oxford, 1994.

Morton, A. L. *A People's History of England.* New York: International, 1968.

Pindell, Terry. *Making Tracks: An American Rail Odyssey.* New York: Grove, 1990.

Postgate, Raymond. *Story of the Year 1848.* New York: Oxford, 1956.

Stampp, Kenneth M. *The Peculiar Institution.* New York: Knopf, 1956.

Stover, John F. *American Railroads.* Chicago: University of Chicago, 1997.

————. *The Routledge Historical Atlas of the American Railroads.* New York: Routledge, 1999.

Takaki, Ronald. *A Different Mirror: A History of Multicultural America.* Boston: Little Brown, 1993.

Wallace, Paul A. W. *Pennsylvania: Seed of a Nation.* New York: Harper, 1962.

Westwood, J. N. *Endurance and Endeavour: Russian History: 1812–1971.* New York: Oxford, 1981.

Williams, William Appleman. *The Contours of American History.* Cleveland: World, 1961.

Wilson, Mitchell A. *American Science and Invention: A Pictorial History.* New York: Simon & Schuster, 1954.

Zinn, Howard. *A People's History of the United States, 1492–Present.* New York: Harper, 1980.

Photo Credits

Photos courtesy of:

American School (19th century)/Library of Congress, Washington, D.C., USA/www.bridgeman.co.uk (p. 39).

Bettmann/CORBIS (pp. 9, 18, 23, 27, 35, 44, 46–47, 53, 74, 81, 84, 86, 91, 120, 123, 127, 130, 134, cover montage).

David Butow/CORBIS SABA (p. 59).

Central Pacific Railroad Photographic History Museum, © 2004 CPRR.org (pp. 26, 54).

Collection of The New-York Historical Society (p. 38).

CORBIS (pp. 17, 29, 31, 32, 49, 64, 67, 100, 102, 106, 135, cover montage).

Denver Public Library, Western History Collection, Call# X-22223 (p. 62).

John William Dillon: President, John Henry Days/Summers County Convention & Visitors Bureau (p. 88).

Hulton-Deutsch Collection/CORBIS (p. 12).

Library of Congress (pp. 19, 129).

Arthur W. V. Mace; Milepost 92 ½/CORBIS (iii, cover main image).

Mary Evans Picture Library (pp. 4, 7, 79, 82, 104, 111, 113, 132, 133, 137, 141).

Frances G. Mayer/CORBIS (p. 76).

National Archives and Records Administration (p. 13).

Newberry Library (p. 107).

North Wind Picture Archives (pp. 15, 22, 43, 45, 51, 55, 56, 69, 80).

Ira Nowinski/CORBIS (p. 139).

Picture Collection, The Branch Libraries, The New York Public Library, Astor, Lenox, and Tilden Foundations (p. 117).

PictureHistory (pp. 72, 98, 109).

Royalty-Free/CORBIS (p. x).

Underwood & Underwood/CORBIS (p. 21, cover montage).

Index

Page numbers in *italics* refer to illustrations.

About the Author

MILTON MELTZER HAS WRITTEN MORE THAN ONE HUNDRED BOOKS FOR young people and adults in the fields of history, biography, and social issues. His many awards and honors include the 2001 Laura Ingalls Wilder Medal as well as the Regina Medal, both given to honor his "substantial and lasting contribution to children's literature." Five of his books have been finalists for the National Book Award. Many of his books have been chosen for the honor lists of the American Library Association, the National Council of Teachers of English, and the National Council for the Social Studies, as well as for the *New York Times* Best Books of the Year list.

Meltzer and his wife, Hildy, live in New York City. He is a member of the Authors Guild, American PEN, and the Organization of American Historians.